Your Mind is Magic
A Guide to Maintaining Positive Thinking

SaBrina Fisher Reece

Copyright 2020 by SaBrina Fisher Reece
Los Angeles, California
All rights reserved
Printed and bound in the United States of America

Published And Distributed by
Impact Publishing
Los Angeles, California
In59Seconds@yahoo.com

Packaging/Consulting
Professional Publishing House
1425 W. Manchester Ave. Ste B
Los Angeles, California 90047
323-750-3592
Email: professionalpublishinghouse@yahoo.com
www.ProfessionalPublishingHouse.com

Cover Design: Joi Spears
Graphic art created by: Joi Spears
First printing March 2021
978-1-7365592-1-7 (hardback)
978-1-7365592-0-8 (paperback)

No part of this book may be reproduced, stored in a retrieval system, or transmitted in any form or by any means without the prior written permission of the author and publisher, except by a reviewer who may quote brief passages in a review to be printed in a newspaper, magazine, or journal. For inquiry, contact the author at: In59Seconds@yahoo.com

Dedication

I dedicate this book to all who may have suffered from depression because they did not know that they were great, to every person, who did not recognize their value, to all who may have endured trauma and are stuck there, unable to move forward from those horrible moments for years, and to all human beings who can benefit from a reminder; You are phenomenal creations of God with a specific purpose here on Earth.

I wrote this book to bring joy, peace, and love to the hearts of those who have forgotten their worth. You are loved, you are worthy of happiness, success, great health, and peace. As long as you have breath in your body, you can accomplish absolutely anything. Your mind is the tool you will need to develop in order to come into your power. *Your Mind is Magic*, and I wrote this book to remind you that each of you matter individually. You are a significant piece to God's amazing puzzle, and I hope that this book reminds you of your value.

About the Author

SaBrina Fisher Reece has earned the title of America's #1 Transformational Mindset Coach from her years of uplifting others through her motivational speaking. She is the author of the popular self-help book, *My Spiritual Smile: Tools for Mental and Emotional Transformation*. She is also the creator of the #In59Seconds Movement which teaches others to uplift, motivate, and encourage themselves and others.

SaBrina owned and operated Inked 4 Life Tattoo Studio and Braids By SaBrina braiding salon and school in Los Angeles, California, for over twenty-four years. Her salon gave her the opportunity to inspire the thousands of young people who worked for her. Not only did she teach them skills that would allow them to support their families financially, but also encouraged them to open their own businesses. After going through her own emotional and spiritual transformation, she was able to share those transformative tools with others.

SaBrina is the mother of four amazing children, and is determined to leave a legacy for the generations that follow her. She considers it a gift to be able to teach others the tools and techniques that can spare them decades of mental and emotional suffering. Her motto is, "Your life is like a coloring book and only you have the crayons, so design the life you desire."

Table of Contents

Mind is All 11

The Real Secret 17

Spend Time with Your Mind 31

Your Imagination is a Gift 45

Fake it until you Feel it 65

It's All Possible 77

Close your Eyes and Visualize 95

Unexpected Journey 113

Recognize Reject Replace 133

Spirituality and Sexuality 153

Subconscious Reprogramming Made Simple 181

The Power of Effective Prayer 195

External circumstances can only cause you physical pain.
Suffering is created in your mind.
-Sadhguru

Chapter 1
Mind is All

The one significant thing we were never taught in school was that our mind controls our lives. Yes, your MIND. What does that even mean? Aren't the mind and the brain the same thing?

The brain and the mind differ greatly. The mind is not tangible matter. There is no mind to cut open and dissect. The brain, however, is tangible, and has been explored by scientists for many years. Yet so many people still question which one is most important.

All of our senses are directly connected to the brain. When you are in physical pain, it is your nervous system that receives and delivers that information to the brain. Your brain is divided into the right and left hemispheres, as well as the frontal, temporal, parietal, and occipital lobes. Each lobe of the brain was designed for its own specific purpose. The brain is so vital, there is more focus on it than the mind. You cannot dissect the mind of a human being as you can the brain. You cannot physically cut open one's mind and study it, but in my opinion the true essence of who we are is because of this intangible mind. We can't see it, but we all have a mind; a voice inside of us that speaks to and guides us. It's how God communicates to us. Many believe it is the origin of our soul. The mind is what makes each and every one of us individuals. For the most part, human brains are all constructed the exact same way. Each mind, however, vastly differs from the other. Just like fingerprints no one's mind is the same.

Our mind houses our individual thoughts. Through the use of our mind we make choices on how we react to life's experiences. When someone makes us angry, the decision is made in our mind to react in an angry manner. There is no objective display that appears before us and says, "It's time to be mad." We make those choices internally via our minds. The same goes for love and kindness. When the emotion of another suddenly strikes you and you decide to be generous and buy a homeless person a meal or give a young striving person a one-hundred dollar bill, the decision to do so happens inside of you. The action is overt, but the choice to do so isn't. It appears that all of the true significant battles all begin in the mind. We decide if something is logical or reasonable in our minds first before we outwardly react. The mind governs all of our actions. The negotiations begin within. In the case of people who appear to be primarily reactive and impulsive, I do not believe they take those few moments to consult their mind first. They simply react, and that impulsive reaction may not have always been the correct choice. Anger and happiness are both choices that begin in the mind. We can control our minds, as opposed to allowing them to control us.

Do you want to be happy? Happiness begins in the mind. The journey to personal development and living our best lives begins inside. Mind is all. Everything begins there. It is the key to perfect health and abundant wealth and everything else we desire. Learning to properly manipulate our minds is the true key to happiness. Yes we can change our minds. Our thoughts are the missing piece to this creative puzzle. We think thousands of thoughts daily, so many we could not even begin to count them. Counting them is not important but monitoring them is. Teaching ourselves to switch negative thoughts into positive ones is crucial. Learning to maintain a positive thinking pattern is the first step to experiencing the best that life has to offer. All human beings can have a wonderful life.

Having a great life is possible if you accept responsibility for your mind. Like a child, we should never allow our minds to run around unattended. Children need our parental guidance to grow and develop. The mind is the same. It is just like our child we have to mold and shape. We must guide our mind in the direction of greatness so that we can experience life abundantly. If we don't direct our mind it will direct us. We must steer that ship in our favor. If we do not, tumultuous seas are ahead. We do not have to accept whatever life brings to us. We can use our amazing beautiful minds to carefully direct our thoughts to ensure that we live up to our fullest capabilities and enjoy the world while doing so.

Limitations are illusions. The only limits that truly exist are the ones you accept in your mind.
-SaBrina Fisher Reece

Chapter 2

The Real Secret

The Mind is not limited. With our minds we can imagine anything we desire. Most people believe the big "secret" of success and happiness is detailed and complicated. I believe the true secret is simple: We control our lives with our thoughts and imagination. Through proper use of the imagination, we can bring forth in our lives anything we desire. This is "The Secret." While humans spend billions of dollars and hours of priceless time searching for the secret to mankind, I sincerely believe it's as simple as controlling our reality through our thoughts. Good thoughts produce a good life and bad thoughts produce a bad life. You may not be able to see the Mind but learning to use this invisible power is very important.

I have studied many different religions, ancient philosophers, and various schools of thought. One conclusion I have found is, many of the people that came long before us knew the importance of focusing our thoughts. Somehow, this information got lost. The more I study great people from the past. I realize this knowledge was known and practiced by many. Long before "thinking positive" became a popular fad, it was a known practice of the ancestors.

Thinking positive on purpose can reshape our lives in a favorable direction. Creating internal visual images of our desires in our minds first allows them to become a reality. Neville Goddard says "Our Imagination is God," working with us and through us, allowing us to be a co-creator of our own lives. I am in agreement with Neville on this subject. Our imagination is the tool we can use to bring our desires into reality.

It is through our intentional focused thought and creating a mental image that all things come into existence. You can call this focused thought prayer, imagination, meditation, stillness or mindfulness. It does not matter how you choose to describe it, as long as you come to realize that your thoughts design your life. Yes! This is very important information. The thoughts in your mind create the reality in your tangible life. For those who sincerely believe that life "just happens," I understand why this would be a difficult concept to grasp, but it is true. It may not seem logical to some, but it is definitely the powerful energy that miracles are made of. The legendary Albert Einstein knew the importance of using our minds to imagine when he said, "Logic will get you from A to Z but imagination will get you everywhere". He went on to stress to the world that "Imagination is more important than knowledge. Knowledge is limited. Imagination encircles the world." I elaborate more on the proper use of imagination in chapter 4.

Our minds will attempt to imagine an equal number of negative things. We must control what we imagine. If we allow persistent negative thoughts to occupy space in our minds, we will continue to experience negative situations in our lives. Once we learn to change those negative thoughts to positive thoughts, we will see our lives take a significant turn for the better.

Take control of your thoughts and drive them down the road you want your life to go down. If you do this, you will have a better life experience. Anything you can imagine will become a reality. This is a power given to us by God. Use this power to create a better life. We do not have to settle for a mediocre existence we can all experience the best life has to offer. This is not an exclusive pleasure. The great pleasures of this earth are not saved for a limited few. With proper use of the mind, everyone can live a prosperous, fulfilling life. Wealth, great health, success and happiness are here for us all. Every human being can experience the wonderful pleasures of life.

So, how do we control our thoughts? This seems especially difficult since we seem to have thousands of them every minute. How could one ever control them? The simplest answer is by being still long enough to monitor them. Sit still even for five minutes a day. Only then will you be able to identify the negative thoughts. Push those thoughts right out of your head and replace them with more positive thoughts.

I understand this is easier said than done, but I assure you with daily practice it can become a habit. Most of us are well into our thirties and or forties before we begin to realize our thoughts make a difference in our lives. Be patient but consistent with the process. Begin by simply writing down the clear and obvious negative thoughts you recognize. Once you identify them. Start working on each one individually. Sometimes, if you take a moment to think about each one you can find the root of where this negative idea began. For example, if someone in your family died of a particular disease and you remember hearing about and fearing this disease as a child. This is the root of how you formed negative thoughts and fears about this specific illness. It does not have to happen to you. Getting this disease is not an unavoidable certainty. You can reprogram your mind regarding the fear associated with contracting and dying from that disease or any disease for that matter.

As we travel throughout life, we form many beliefs that do not promote a great life. Let's say when you were five years old, your parents had a friend who died in a plane crash. This incident was very traumatic for your parents. You watched them grieve and cry. You even attended the funeral with them. Being too young to fully comprehend the death, all you saw was pain and sadness associated with airplanes. This is precisely where the negative seed was planted and this sparked your fear of flying. These subconscious fears can lay dormant within us for years until something triggers them. It takes intentional, focused quiet time to recognize these triggers and itemize their individual root causes. Although there are incidents throughout our lives that cause us to have certain fears, we do not have to continue to live with them and allow them to affect our lives. We can identify them and change them. You cannot change or reprogram any negative thinking patterns until you realize they exist. The ability to recognize them is a gift. Spend time with your mind. Take a moment to understand which thoughts need to be reversed. Make it your mission to begin the reversal process.

The mind is everything. Without the proper use of the mind, we leave our lives subject to chance. If we are unaware that we have the ability to choose our thoughts, then we will allow all thoughts to run rampant in our mind. We tend to underestimate the magnitude of damage negative thoughts can have. Continuing to allow negative thoughts to take up space in our mind is detrimental to the quality of life we live. Imagine happiness. Imagine wealth. Imagine perfect health. Each one of these is possible for everyone. Take a mere five minutes a day to close your eyes and imagine the life you desire. Begin to feel the visual as reality and soon it will be.

The truth is, your mind is magic, and you possess the magic wand. You are in control. You can guide your mind in any direction you choose. That is the wonderful secret that seems to have gotten lost as time progressed. However, many of our ancestors were privy to this power. This amazing gift is extremely powerful, so we must realize what a huge responsibility God has given us.

The mind is a non-judgmental garden. If you plant seeds of negativity and doubt that is exactly what will grow. On the other hand if you plant positive seeds, seeds of greatness, seeds of love, seeds of kindness then your garden will produce just that. So, it's truly all in your hands. This magic I speak of is non-bias. It won't tell you, "No, I refuse to produce this because it's not going to enhance your life." If you plant it, it will grow.

That analogy alone was enough for me to aggressively begin working on my M.I.N.D. techniques. I developed this acronym to help me remember the importance of the mind and maintaining a positive mental attitude.

MIND
M - Manipulating
I - Ideas in a
N - New
D - Direction

Learning to manipulate our ideas in a new direction was the main goal in writing this book. Yes! This helped me to control my mind's magic. If I was attending an event and I walked into the room feeling insecure because of recent weight gain, or maybe my skin wasn't at its best, instead of allowing the idea that other people in that room noticed my flaws to persist in my mind, I would change it to a different idea. I would say, "I am beautiful, people are staring at me because I look amazing today." Choosing to change my interpretation of others' glances changed my experience at the event, and as a result I enjoyed myself without allowing my mind to rob me of having a good time. We have no way of truly knowing what a person is thinking when they look our way, so why not choose to perceive the look as something coming from a positive place. Isn't that a more pleasant option.? Now, if I am concerned about an event I'm about to attend, I take a few minutes to meditate and visualize the exact way I want things to turn out. I create situations in my mind that make me feel loved. For example, I imagine everyone telling me how amazing I look and how gorgeous my dress is. In my mind, I create the entire day just as I desire it to be. If I want to be the center of attention, then I create that scenario in my mind. Taking the time to practice these imagination techniques makes it so much easier for me to enter the room. It's our world and we create our realities.

I remember being terribly nervous about giving a speech for my Eastern Star organization. Although I had been speaking professionally for a few years, this speech had me quite unsettled. I was the current Grand OES Queen for the year 2017 of the Golden State Grand Chapter, Order of the Eastern Star, Prince Hall Rite of Adoption for the state of California. This was my going-out queen speech. The crowning of the new queen would take place later that day. Because I had not felt completely embraced by some of the women in the organization, I was terribly afraid to deliver this speech. Most of the members had never heard me speak before, so I just didn't know what to expect. Being the determined person I am, I would not back out no matter how uneasy I felt. The day before my speech, I did nothing but visualize the outcome I desired. I closed my eyes and saw myself on stage in my beautiful white queen dress and sparkly queen's crown, delivering a magnificent, inspirational speech. I created the image of the audience in my mind. I visualized the event going exactly as I wanted it to. In my visual, the audience members were smiling and clapping, fully receiving the message I was delivering, even laughing at my jokes. Creating that visual helped me tremendously. If there were any non-supportive people in the audience, I didn't even notice them. I chose to design the room the way I wanted it to be and lived completely in my desired image of the moment and the moment became a reality. It all worked out perfectly! Creative visualization works! The ability to believe in things unseen is a tool God gave to us. The speech was a great success. I'd honestly had more fun that day as the outgoing queen than I did as the incoming queen.

It truly is all in the mind. Everything begins and ends there. Most of the situations we fear and torment ourselves with never actually happen anywhere but in our own minds. We have all been guilty of this, but it is time to fully understand the damage we do to our lives by allowing these negative thinking patterns to continue. Ask yourself why we tend to think about failure, death and tragedy far more often than they actually happen. We must learn to catch our mind when it is stuck focusing on imaginary situations that are not positive. Earl Nightingale said, "Whatever we plant into our subconscious mind and nourish with repetition and emotion will become a reality".

It may seem difficult at first to monitor every single thought, but it will eventually become second nature. Practicing it daily will make it easier and effortless eventually. I have been doing it for so long now my mind instantly begins reciting positive affirmations as soon as I wake up. Soon you will see your entire life change. The mind is amazing, and once you realize that the true key to happiness, success, great health, wealth, and all the love you desire all start with the mind, you will become dedicated to monitoring and manipulating your thoughts.

Practice it as you would anything in your life that you want to master. I create mental exercises regularly to help hone my creative visualization skills. Start with simple ones. If you are dating someone who you sincerely want to marry. Create a visual of them standing at the altar waiting for you with a huge smile on their face. Imagine them walking toward you with a loving gaze, eager to become your life partner. Visualize your friends and family hugging you and your new spouse after the wedding during the reception. Imagine them all smiling and wishing the newly married couple well. Then imagine a happy marriage. Literally create mental images of the two of you celebrating your fifth, tenth and twenty-fifth anniversary. Design the entire relationship exactly the way you desire it to be. If you want your mate to give you lavish gifts several times a year, create that picture in your mind. Imagine a huge smile on your face as you graciously thank him/her for the gifts. Allow yourself to actually feel the feelings of gratitude while receiving them. These mental exercises work.

Commit to five minutes twice a day to intentionally creating positive images in your head. The image will become clearer and clearer each time. Once you have mastered the visual, add emotion to it. Emotion is the icing on the cake. Try to feel the way you would feel if this was actually happening. Combine the visual with the emotion and you have a perfect recipe for manifestation. Conscious, positive thought combined with feeling and emotion are the real secret to creating a great life.

You have power over your mind, not outside events. Realize this, and you will find strength.

-Marcus Aurelius

Chapter 3

Spend Time with Your Mind

For us to become aware of our thoughts we first need to slow our lives down a bit. We must take advantage of quiet moments and be still long enough to monitor our thoughts. When you are sitting in traffic, turn the radio off, take a few deep breaths, and begin to notice and acknowledge every thought that comes into your mind. Learning to do this changed my life tremendously. Both good and bad thoughts need recognition. You cannot reverse negative thoughts if you have not taken the time to recognize and acknowledge they exist. Begin by keeping it as simple as taking a mental note of what you are thinking. Start by observing exactly what you are thinking right now. Take ten minutes and detach from everything in the world except your thoughts. Make a conscious decision to do this every day and, eventually you will see the clear distinction between intentional thoughts versus when our mind runs rampant on its own without any guidance from us. Only then will you notice how many thoughts of fear and impending tragedy run through our minds. These are specifically the thoughts we must learn to dismiss. These are the thoughts that will ultimately cause us harm.

It's not horrible to admit you have negative thoughts, on the contrary, it's the first step to a better life. Many will spend years in complete denial. Denying they are even capable of thinking negatively. Negative thoughts exist, just like crime, and while we may not be able to control the crime in the world, we have the power to monitor our thoughts. Stop judging your thoughts as good or bad and re-label them as "thoughts that make you feel good" or "thoughts that make you feel bad." Choosing to label them as good or bad will make you less likely to acknowledge the ones that are not in line with what you desire for your life. Denial and embarrassment will slow down the process. We all think negatively at times. No need to guilt yourself for being a bad thinker. We all have thoughts of fear, failure, anger, sickness, and sadness. You are not alone. You are not a bad person for thinking that way. However, now that you are aware of the damage sustaining a negative thinking pattern can do to your life, it's time to change it. Feel good about being at a place in your life where you are willing to make positive changes towards the betterment of your future. This is the best gift you can give to yourself and others. Learning how to control and change your thoughts will change your life.

As human beings we can get so distracted by the ins and outs of our daily routines that most of us rarely even realize that we are thinking all day. Scientists say we have twelve to sixty thousand thoughts per day. Thoughts come continuously, whether or not we choose to guide them. These thoughts are shaping our daily lives so we must learn to take charge of them. You are what you think all day long. There is no way around it. Our realities are shaped solely by our thoughts. If it's present in our lives, even if we don't remember those specific thoughts, we did indeed think them. We have to learn to create barriers to keep the negative thoughts from penetrating our subconscious mind.

We can't avoid thinking, so it's best we take control over this imminent process and manipulate it in our favor. All thoughts travel on energetic frequencies. We are energy as well. Everything in this world is energy, and we have the power to control the energy we put out. Energy exists, no matter what, but we can determine if the energy we emit is positive or negative. If we are entertaining thoughts of disease because someone we know was just diagnosed with an illness and we are now in fear of getting it, then rest assured that our energetic vibration is low at that time. The good thing is we are in control of the level of energy we put out. We can raise our own energetic vibration at any time.

A friend of mine taught me about saging a few years ago. At that point in my life, I was open to new ideas and concepts regarding religion and spirituality. She brought a small piece of sage to my salon and showed me how to use it. I am a person that knows the importance of "belief" in something, so as she was showing me how to rid my body and private spaces of negative energy that can lurk in corners and dark spaces, I set a conscious intention to not reject what she was saying simply because it was foreign to me. Even though it was different and conflicted with my childhood Christian beliefs, I tried to listen and learn with an open mind. I decided that day that the practice of saging was no different than the Christian ritual of taking communion. The drinking of the grape juice and eating of the cracker is also a ritual in remembrance of Jesus Christ and his bodily sacrifice. Communion is a ritual that Christians chose to assign symbolism to. Unfortunately, it was my experience growing up in COGIC (Church Of God in Christ) that only our rituals were accepted, and everything else was considered voodoo or witchcraft. I no longer believe that. I can't say I ever personally bought into the voodoo concept; it was simply the belief of many of the elders that came before me. Most were devout Christians and would have never accepted the belief in healing crystals, burning sage and meditation to open our chakras. Chakras are the centers of spiritual power in the human body. After my friend was gone I decided to practice what she taught me about saging. I also chose to envision the dark energy leaving through a window and the positive energy coming in. I would say "Negative energy out, positive energy in." As I walk around my salon burning the sage and setting my intentions for positivity and prosperity, I would close my eyes and believe it all as fact. What you believe is what truly matters. You can practice certain rituals but inside you have no faith in them, so they won't work. Many people believe the art of rituals and spiritual ceremonies are evil and demonic. My response to people who say that to me is "That's not what it means to me". Do not allow other people to assign an intention to something you choose to do. For example I am a mother of four and I would allow my children to dress up in customs for Halloween and take part in the parade at school. We would even go from house to house trick- or treating in the evening. Frequently people have reminded me of some ancient original demonic meaning the Halloween holiday. It never bothered me one bit because that is not what me and my children celebrate it for. We have no evil intent behind our choice to celebrate the holiday nor are we bound by anyone else's. There is always someone who chooses to corrupt something. I choose to see the positive in all things. And any holiday that promotes love and brings people and families closer is OK with me. The choice to participate in something evil is just that, a choice. I'm not interested, and it has nothing to do with me.

The practice of saging became a regular practice in my salon, Braids By SaBrina, which has been my sole source of income for twenty-five years. In September 2019, I changed the name of my salon to "A New Vision Dreadlock Studio."

One would think changing the name of a popular business that had serviced the Los Angeles community for so long would not be a great idea, but I sat in stillness for a while and the new name suddenly came to me in less than fifteen minutes. I was fifty years old. I had recently dealt with some unexpected medical issues that caused me to rethink allowing any form of stress in my life. My staff at my salon were a key source of stress, and at this point there wasn't much of a financial benefit to keeping them around. I felt I had given all that I could to them over the years and now I had to make myself and my health a priority. I made an instant decision to terminate them and change the name of the salon to "A New Vision Dreadlock Studio." It was a new day and time for A New Vision as I embarked upon the second half of my life. To this day, I have never regretted my decision. The new salon name came to me so peacefully that I knew it was God telling me to move forward. When we spend time with our mind we will discover answers to questions, solutions to problems will be revealed to us. I started sitting quietly in the empty salon; something I was never able to do when I had employees. I would visualize abundant wealth, and thank God for continued success. I spoke aloud words of gratitude for my business and how consistent it had been. Then I would walk from room to room, saging my beautiful purple salon and speaking my affirmations for both my business and myself aloud. I raised my personal prices considerably and within thirty days of rebranding my salon, I was making double what I made before, even without having a staff. It turned out to be one of the best decisions I have ever made.

Wealth and success can become a reality for anyone who sincerely believes it is possible. I believe that is why I have never experienced poverty. I expect wealth, and yes, I advertise and do all the footwork needed to sustain a small business, but that to me is secondary. My belief that the business could not fail was the primary cause of its continued success. Advertising and promoting a business won't work if subconsciously you believe it will fail. We must see the success in our mind first. God gave us this power as a gift to mankind, but most do not use it. You can experience success in all areas of your life if you first believe it to be possible. All things are possible!. This new practice of saging was just another tool I used to set intentions for peace and prosperity in my life. There is not one specific tool. Any practice you put complete unwavering belief in will be successful.

I'm pleased that I opened my mind and allowed myself to at least listen to other concepts and beliefs and make my own choices. Having that open mind allowed me to be more receptive when I traveled to Bali, Indonesia, Cusco, Peru, Cairo, Egypt, Istanbul, Turkey, and Athens, Greece. In these countries, I visited many monasteries and spiritual temples, which helped to strengthen my belief in one Divine Source.

Different people may package God differently. They may refer to God with a different name, but to me, it's all the same. I respect the amount of reverence that other countries give to honor the creator. I have partaken in many rituals and ceremonies that greatly differ from my Christian church practices. What I've learned is to allow others to worship God the way they choose. It's not my business. If there was a particular practice that resonated with me, I adopted it as my own and moved forward. I feel we get so distracted in pointing out the different way in which we all choose to acknowledge God. Our ego wants us to be correct. It convinces us that our way is the only way. It's a distraction and a judgement that I don't believe in. To each his own. Who are we to say how another person should acknowledge God? The ultimate universal goal is to live a great life. Learning, growing and evolving in all areas and allowing others to do the same.

I do, however, believe that once we fully evolve we don't necessarily need to practice daily rituals to remind us to be positive and speak positivity over our lives. By then, the positive thought process will have become second nature. However, until then, the daily practices that help us keep a positive mental attitude are crucial to having a productive life. They help us form positive daily habits. I was proud that I was able to open my mind and embrace practices that were a definite step out of the C.O.G.I.C. box I was raised in. I have gotten to a point where I enjoy them. I believe strongly in them. I believe they are necessary, and I look forward to doing them daily. I still believe very much in Jesus Christ. I believe he was here to teach us of our Amazing internal power. I believe that power is what he was referring to as "The Kingdom of Heaven" with-in us all. I will always be eternally grateful for my Christian upbringing. Unlike most I see correlations between Christianity and spirituality. I combine what practices and beliefs work best for my life and move forward.

I have convinced myself that taking that small time out of my day to speak positivity over my body, my family, my business, and my life in general is truly the reason I no longer suffer from many of the things a lot of people in this world currently suffer with. I want to teach others how I rid my life of sadness, pain, hopelessness and depression. I get so excited about teaching these practices to others because it is my desire for everyone to learn that their happiness is a choice, and choosing to spend just a little time with your mind can ensure you live a better life.

Your Mind is Magic

As far as we know, we only get one mind. Spend as much time with it as possible. View your mind as the cockpit of an airplane. With all the controls clearly accessible and you are the pilot.

@In59Seconds

Forgiveness frees the heart and mind, and prepares you for greatness.
-SaBrina Fisher Reece

CHAPTER 4

Your Imagination Is A Gift

One of the most precious gifts God gave us other than life is our ability to imagine. God gave us the ultimate control over the outcome of our lives through our imagination. I realize that initially it's a hard concept to grasp, but it's true. If we can imagine it, we can have it. It is through the use of these amazing imaginations of ours that we can live our best lives.

When you watch small children closely, you will see that they possess the untainted ability to imagine. They play for hours on end with people we can't see. They invent them in their minds, and if we truly watch them, it seems natural to them to create these playmates. I believe it is our natural ability to create, believe in, and interact with the unseen. As we age, we grow further and further away from our natural instincts. It seems to be the one missing piece from most lives.

Like me, most people have no idea that their imagination has the power to create. I definitely did not know that when I was younger, nor did I have the slightest clue that I had any control over what I imagined. I now know that we can change and manipulate that visual. I still catch myself when my mind gets stuck on a visualization that isn't positive. Many times, I'll imagine one of my kids getting hurt, or I will create negative conversations with people in my mind. The difference between the old me and the new me is once I realize I am creating that negativity in my mind, I immediately stop it. That's the first step. I'll sometimes physically shake my head to rid my mind of the negative movie playing inside, and instead of berating myself for allowing the negative thought to happen, I applaud myself for catching it and casting it out. When I speak to others motivationally, I teach a "Catch and Cast" technique. Catch the negative thoughts and cast them out.

The gift of imagination is powerful. In our mind we can literally design the exact picture of the life we desire to live. Whatever we allow our minds to focus on will eventually transform into matter and become tangible. Just try it! Take five minutes daily and focus on having a new car. In your mind's eye, design the vehicle to the very last detail. See the color, the make and model with every detail you want. Imagine everything from the steering wheel to the tires. Visualize the color of the seats and the carpet on the floor. Then imagine yourself sitting in it smiling, feeling so grateful for this new, beautiful car.

The magic of creation happens when we combine the image we have created with the emotion of receiving it. Neville Goddard said, "Imagination is the very gateway of reality."

We must practice using our imagination in a positive way. Do this daily, even if it's for only a few minutes, and you will improve your life. The amount of time that it takes the things you desire to manifest is determined by how quickly you are able to completely remove doubt from the visuals you are creating. Doubt and fear counteract the manifestation. Pretend that you have it already. Believe that it exists in the present time and it will. I'm positive this is what the Bible was referring to in the scripture, "Believe in things unseen as if they already are."

Often, you will hear someone who has attained success in some area say, "I never imagined that this would happen to me." I'd like to challenge them by convincing them that it would not be happening had they not imagined it. At some point they must have held that thought in their mind for it to take root and grow into reality. The president of the United

States would not have become president had he not mentally seen himself in that position. Singers would not be on stage singing had they not once visualized themselves there. The thoughts that we focus on are the ones that manifest into reality. It is important that we intentionally imagine the life we desire. Recognize the imagination for the gift of creation that it is.

Keep in mind, your imagination can bring your negative thoughts into reality as well. Try not to spend an extended amount of time imagining bad things. When you notice that you are daydreaming and it's not a good dream, stop it in its tracks and intentionally imagine something that makes you happy. We have so many unfounded subconscious fears that we don't realize how much we sit and think about things like death, car accidents, heartache, etc. Make sure your positive thoughts outweigh your negative. God gave us the power to bring things into existence. Make sure the things you bring into your life are good things.

Once you finally accept you do have this power, you will be more mindful of monitoring your thinking patterns. I can't say it's easy to continuously monitor your thoughts, but it will prove to be worth the effort and eventually it will become easier to do. Anything you do daily will become a habit. It should be everyone's goal to make positive thinking a habit.

Consider the quiet times you have to just sit and breathe and access your thoughts as a gift, because a gift is exactly what these moments are; a wonderful opportunity to take charge and be solely responsible for your happiness. We spend years blaming others for how our lives turn out, but rarely do we take responsibility for not making use of our divine God-given power to design a better life. Accepting this power does not negate the hurt that we have suffered at the hands of others. It doesn't erase injustices or minimize inequalities in the world. It simply frees us from the bondage of being a victim to the pain and trauma we have endured for the rest of our lives.

I don't believe in classifying people as good or bad because there is negative and positive in us all. However, this amazing power to create and manifest our desires is not only given to those the world perceives as good. Mind Magic is for everyone. We can choose to use it for good or evil. Keep in mind that humans are subject to certain immutable laws, so if you use your power to create chaos or evil, it will come back to you. Like attracting like is a universal law of karma that we seem to have no control over. It's simple, the energy you put out into the universe will return to you.

On my journey for truth I have studied many different interpretations of Universal Law. Some say there are seven or eight. Some say ten to fourteen with only a few of them being immutable. Immutable laws are the laws that we cannot change, such as gravity. Whether you are a good person or a bad person, if you decide to jump off of a building, due to the immutable law of gravity, you will go down and most likely not survive the fall. According to Newton, "What goes up, must come down." We don't know why this is, but as it stands it's a reality and a law we can't change.

Universal Laws are laws that were not made by man. They are laws that govern our universe:

15 Universal Laws

- The Law of Oneness
- The Law of Vibration
- The Law of Gravity
- The Law of Action (Action is energy in motion)
- The Law of Cause and Effect (Every action has a reaction or consequence)

- The Law of Correspondence (As above, so below; As within so without)
- The Law of Compensation
- The Law of Attraction (Like attracts like)
- The Law of Perpetual Transmutation of Energy (We have the power to change the energy in our lives)
- The Law of Gestation (Everything has its time to manifest)
- The Law of Relativity (Each person will receive challenges to strengthen them, it's all relative)
- The Law of Polarity (Everything has an opposite)
- The Law of Rhythm (Everything vibrates and moves)
- The Law of Belief (What you believe with thought & emotion will become reality)
- The Law of Gender (Yin & Yang; everything has masculine and feminine energy)

Some believe there are only seven universal laws. These are the seven deemed most important. These laws are also referred to as the "Seven Hermetic Laws" in the Kybalion.

7 Laws Universal Laws

1. The Law of Mentalism (Everything is mental. Everything originates from universal mind)
2. The Law of Correspondence (As above, so below; As within, so without. There is harmony and agreement between the spiritual and physical realms)
3. The Law of Attraction (We are magnets, and we attract everything that matches our intention and the energy we emit)
4. The Law of Polarity (Everything is dual. All truths are but half-truths, opposites are the same, but vary in degree)
5. The Law of Rhythm (Everything flows, rises and falls)
6. The Law of Cause and Effect (Karma; For every action there is a consequence)
7. The Law of Gender (Gender manifests on all planes. Within every woman lies all the latent qualities of a man, and vice versa)

It took me years to fully understand these laws and even longer to decide that I believed in them, but they answer a lot of questions we have in life. Times when things just seem to happen no matter what we do. When we realize we are all subjected to these universal laws, things make a little more sense. I began to study the Law of Polarity, realizing that all opposites exist simultaneously. I made a point to be more intentional on which side of the pole I wanted to operate on. It also made me less judgmental in labeling others as either good or bad. I realized how close we all are to the opposite and how easily we can cross the center and move and operate on the other side of the pole. It all comes down to a choice. Good or bad, right or wrong, love or hate, we choose how we want to be.

We may try to be positive, but sometimes anger can cause us to swing to the opposite side and become negative. It's a choice to what degree and for how long we stay on the other side of the pole, but understanding polarity helps you see that we all start in the center. We choose to advance to one side or the other. And even when we swing to the less favorable side we can always come back.

It's also quite comforting once you fully understand the Law of Rhythm. You realize that when things seem low they will rise. There is a natural eb and flow. According to this law, all things rise and fall. This law is helpful when trying to understand the importance of balance. During times in your life when all seems to be going haywire, take comfort in knowing that according to the universal law of rhythm, things will get better. These Laws are things that may take what seems like a lifetime to comprehend, but I'm committed to doing so because all things mental, physical, and spiritual appear to be connected. And understanding that connection can lead to a more harmonious life.

When I was younger and knew nothing of vibration or frequency. I'm sure I was always vibrating low. I would get angry and sad a lot. I suffered from depression, and I had no idea I had any control over how I felt. Knowing the things I know now could have definitely minimized my suffering as a young adult. Now, I rarely find myself in those dark places. It's not that the feelings of sadness and despair don't show up periodically. I simply know exactly what to do to immediately get rid of them, or as I now refer to it, "raise my vibration." In January 2020, I appeared on a court television show. After it aired in March, I received a lot of ridicule and cruelty via social media. I was devastated at the amount of hurtful messages I received, attacking everything from my personal appearance to my confident demeanor on the show. I could not believe the people went out of their way to contact me with the intent to be negative. The plaintiff and I both were given a fair shot at presenting our cases, and I won the case, fair and square. What was all the negative backlash about? Her dishonest testimony in court resulted in the judge not awarding her one cent. Her negative response later that day online sincerely caught me off guard. I was deeply hurt by the comments and for a minute I began to question my own beauty. My confidence was shaken. I remember walking to a mirror several times, internalizing all of their negative comments wishing I had not read them. I knew this was not positive, yet I had allowed it to get to me and it lowered my vibration. This situation gave me a lot of compassion for celebrities or people in the public eye. No one deserves public ridicule and it is very hurtful. As the world adapts quickly into a virtual society we must learn the art of encouraging ourselves daily so we don't not fall susceptible to online bullies.

I still cry when my feelings are hurt. I guess I just can't understand cruelty. This obvious sensitivity I have to it makes me stay mindful and make sure I do not treat anyone in a cruel way. I think every person should attempt to be kind to others. No one is perfect and we all have days where our spirits are low. However, please make it a point even during those times to be gentle and loving with yourself and others.

Now of course I know the damage of staying in that emotionally low place, so despite the fact that my feelings were deeply hurt and my self-esteem was greatly affected, I had to get up and do the work needed to bring myself back. I needed to speak positive affirmations to myself aloud and in a mirror. I had to encourage myself, as I teach my readers to do, and remind myself of my greatness. It would be great if we were all so evolved that we never allowed the opinions of others to affect us. It sounds good, but we still reside in a human body and can still be emotionally affected by others despite the abundance of mental and emotional work many of us have done. The great thing is, once we have armed ourselves with empowerment tools and the knowledge of how to use them we can always implement positive affirmations, meditation, effective prayer, and creative visualization to rebuild our confidence and return to love. And as hard as it may be, send positive energy and love to those that have harmed you because they are still part of the divine source. God loves them as much as he does you.

Clairaudience

In some way we are all connected spiritually. The idea of being connected to God, the Divine source of us all is quite comforting to me. I have come to believe we all have been given spiritual gifts from God. I can't say I fully understand their purpose, or how they enhance our lives, but I am now certain that I too have a gift. I am not positive, but I believe my spiritual gift is called clairaudience. I realize that some people may find this weird, but these things actually happen to me. On four separate occasions in my life, I have heard clearly and audibly recognizable voices that were not actually there.

1st time: I was twenty-one and my grandmother who raised me from three months to seventeen years old had been killed a few years prior. I was sleeping soundly when I heard her voice say, "Brina." I sat up in my bed peacefully and was so certain that it was her voice. There was no doubt who it was. I didn't for one second think it was anyone else. It was definitely the voice of my grandmother. Surprisingly I was not startled or afraid as many may have been from hearing the voice of a loved one who had passed on. I felt a sense of peace from the voice, and she was the only person in the world, even to this day that calls me Brina. I felt comforted so I lay back down and went back to sleep and never heard her voice again.

2nd time: I was forty-nine years old in 2019. I had been working really hard for the past three days and was sleeping unnaturally hard. I was in that stage of sleep where you're almost awake, but not quite. I clearly and very audibly heard my two youngest children in their room, adjacent to mine, trying to kill something that was on the wall. I don't know if it was a mosquito or what, but I heard them hitting the broom on the wall. I heard Journey, who was five years old at the time, scream to JJ, "Kill it! Did you get it?" I went back to sleep for a few more hours. When I woke up, I called JJ(Jayden) into my room. "What was it you were trying to kill ?" I asked her.

She said, "Huh?" I said, "I heard you and Journey in the room. You guys were making a lot of noise trying to kill something on the ceiling or wall. I heard the broom hitting the ceiling. Journey was screaming "Kill it."

She said, "Mom that was three days ago, and you weren't even home when it happened."

How was I able to tap into the audio of an incident that actually happened in my house three days prior, when I was not even there? How is that possible?

3rd Time: The day my oldest daughter Joi and her family moved to Arizona on Saturday, March 28th 2020. I was doing fine. I had months to accept the fact that she was moving, so I was not as emotionally upset as I expected myself to be, being that she was moving away with my infant first grandchild. We got them all packed and she and her husband and baby left to start their new lives. The evening came and I went to bed. When I woke up that morning, I clearly heard my grandson, Raiden crying as he normally does in the morning. I text Joi and said, "I just heard Raiden crying." She confirmed all the way from Arizona via text that he had just been crying before I texted her.

4th time: April 1, 2020. I was sleeping soundly, because I had been awake from midnight until 4:00 a.m. I woke up by what sounded like Joi walking into my room, saying, "Mom." She sounded sick, like she was coming to tell me she didn't feel good. I Instantly woke up! I texted my daughter in Arizona and asked if she was okay. She jokingly texted back; "Mom tell the ghost in the house to leave you alone."

After the fourth incident I began to study even more spiritual books and videos. I learned that most people have spiritual gifts, but it is our choice whether to ignore these gifts or embrace and develop them. I am still unsure what purpose these gifts have for showing up in our lives but I'm curious to find out. I only want to develop my spiritual gift of clairaudience if it will help me and those close to me advance in some positive way. I have no desire to hear voices for no reason. if it can serve some positive purpose in my life then I'm all for it.

There is one irrefutable certainty in this life. We will all die. Each and every one of us, no matter what great physical condition we are in, or how much energy we have put into gaining wealth and success. We will all leave this life experience at some point. Accepting this makes it easier for me to concern myself less with how, when, and why. Instead, I choose to focus on making sure I leave a significant legacy. I want my children to be able to pick up one of my books and share the beliefs and concepts that were important to me with others. I want them to remember that I taught them that they are creators, and that they are responsible for their own lives. I want them to know the importance of loving themselves first. I want them to create opportunities for themselves and to not accept any limitations. Before I leave this Earth, it is my duty as a parent to make sure they understand that people are not as limited as they sometimes believe they are. They can have whatever life they desire, and I would like to ensure they possess the tools needed to acquire it.

Yes, there are many things we all can do to extend our life experience, but knowing that no matter what, it will end one day should make us all want to commit to making sure we figure out what our true purpose here is, and direct all of our energy toward pursuing it. While pursuing your purpose, make happiness your mission. Enjoy every moment of this beautiful life experience.

Control your mind, or it controls you.
-Napoleon Hill

Chapter 5

Fake It Until You Feel It

We have all heard the phrase, "Fake it until you make it," but I have further expanded on the meaning of that since I have learned the importance of feeling. Now, I choose to say, "Fake it until you feel it." Once we begin utilizing personal development tools like imagination, creative visualization and affirmations, we realize that sometimes when we buckle down to begin the process we aren't always in the best mood. We may be preparing to say the affirmation: "I am happy and healthy, I am happy and healthy," but at that very moment we don't feel happy or healthy. My suggestion is to go stand in front of a mirror and repeat it anyway. Fake the feeling, pretend as children do. As you continue to speak this powerful affirmation to yourself in the mirror repeatedly, you will eventually begin to actually feel that way. The consistent affirmative stance will transform the negative feeling into a positive one. Positivity wins every time.

I realize many of us are quite busy with our lives and do not feel we have time for long drawn out positive affirmation sessions. That is why I created the #In59seconds Movement. A simple 59 seconds each day of positivity can and will change our lives. While you're running around getting dressed to begin your day. Take 59 seconds to speak to the universe. Speak the perfect day you desire into existence. Tell yourself, "I feel great today. Today is beautiful. Today is a happy day. Today I will make a lot of money. Today everyone will be happy to see me." It does not have to consume a lot of your time. Just 59 seconds of uplifting fuel will do the trick. It can be the very boost you need to ensure a productive day. Use that same 59 seconds to encourage others. Tell your children they are amazing and they have the ability to accomplish anything. Tell your spouse how much you appreciate them and how attractive they look today. This small amount of time of positive empowerment can make a difference in your life and the lives of others. The #In59Seconds Movement can motivate the world.

Words are energy and it has been my experience that repeatedly saying an affirmation aloud will eventually invoke the feeling, and the feeling is the last puzzle piece. Just try it, you have absolutely nothing to lose. Once we couple the positive words with the feelings, that is when the magic of manifestation happens. We must combine the consistent speaking of the words with the feeling of actually having what we desire. This is the perfect recipe to create a great life for yourself.

Many unfortunate situations can and will happen in life. When we allow ourselves to feel bad, we lower our energetic vibration. Despite how justified we are in negatively reacting to a bad situation. We still cannot allow ourselves to stay in the negative state of mind. Thinking negatively lowers our energetic vibration. If we are vibrating at a low frequency then we will attract all things that are also vibrating at that low level. That is why it is vital to learn to raise our vibration as soon as we wake up in the morning. We can raise our own vibration and it's imperative that we do so before we leave the house.

Gospel music is a tool I use daily to feel better. Quite often when I wake up in the morning, my mind is instantly flooded with what bills are due, who I'm upset with, who has disappointed me, what responsibilities I have for the day. Yes, It can be overwhelming. But it's crucial that we do not allow those feelings to continue. We can choose to change how we perceive things. Yes, bills and other financial responsibilities exist however we do not have to perceive them as problems. I now train myself to start thanking God that I have a home to pay a mortgage on rather than being annoyed that the mortgage is due. Instead of agonizing over paying my monthly car note, I remind myself that many don't have vehicles and I continuously put my mind in a state of gratitude that I have always been blessed to have a nice one.

We were born with the natural ability to feel good. We produce natural serotonin in our brains. Serotonin is a chemical messenger that is believed to act as a mood stabilizer. It helps us sleep better. Studies show that high serotonin levels are linked to feeling good and living longer, which should be an ultimate goal for us all.

There are certain foods that increase our body's production of serotonin. Specialists in this field encourage people to eat these specific foods that have been proven to raise the level of serotonin in our bodies. According to the expert these foods include eggs, cheese, pineapples, tofu, salmon, nuts and seeds, and turkey. It may be beneficial to study these foods and others that stimulate serotonin production and choose which of these foods fit best into your daily lifestyle.

When our serotonin levels are low, we may feel irritable, anxious, depressed, pessimistic and experience irregular sleeping patterns. On the contrary, when our serotonin levels are high, we feel happy, energized, and hopeful. Doesn't everyone want to feel happy?

Natural ways to increase serotonin include exercise, cold showers, natural sunshine, prayer, meditation, singing, dancing, and speaking positive affirmations. There isn't just one way. Find what tools work for you and what compliments your lifestyle and practice it daily. Do not view this practice as a chore. Allow yourself to view participating in these daily practices as you willfully doing something daily to enhance the quality of your life. Even when you simply don't feel it, fake it! Do it anyway. You would be surprised how quickly your feelings will turn around.

I love working out, but sometimes I am lazy, and I simply do not want to do it. I find that if I force myself to get up anyway, shortly after beginning I start to feel so good about myself. Instantly I'll start to see that I have elevated my mood or raised my vibration by pushing myself to do it anyway. Raising one's vibration simply means choosing to operate at a higher frequency. Being happy versus sad, energetic versus a lack of energy, being hopeful versus choosing to focus on all your problems.

The concept of "fake it until you feel it" in no way means be unauthentic. It plainly means act as if you feel good until you do. Act as if you want to work out and eventually you will be so grateful that you did. Act as if you have abundance in your life and one day you will. Choose to act pleasant in public as opposed to acting grumpy. Get up and go out into the world and act happy and shortly you will forget that you weren't. Most importantly, you will attract others who are attempting to be positive as well.

When we are parents it is vital that we don't bombard our children with negative phrases like, "This is a horrible day," or "Life sucks." They are listening to our every word. Whether we like or not, they are mentally recording the things they hear us say. To me, this is more of a reason to "fake it". Your five-year-old need not hear the doom and gloom of your life. We owe them a fair chance at happiness, and if all they hear from us is a negative picture of the world, they will begin to feel that way themselves, which is grossly unfair to a child. Show them love and smiles, days filled with happiness and joy and they will grow into happy adults.

There is always something to be grateful for, and expressing that gratitude usually makes you feel better. Let gratitude change your attitude, and in doing so you will learn to drop all those negative labels you put on yourself, and soon you will find yourself becoming a cheerful, motivated, and happy person whom others want to be around.

When I first began speaking motivationally, I had absolutely no experience whatsoever. Other than the few speeches I had given in my Toastmasters International Club, I was a complete novice. Despite being a complete beginner, I started branding myself as a successful motivational speaker. I began dressing the part. I had a professional photo shoot done. I dressed like a speaker. When I walked into a room that I was to deliver a speech in, I was always super nervous. My heart felt like it was going to jump out of my chest each time, yet I walked in the room with confidence. I faked it until I felt it. People would compliment me and give me feedback and called me a seasoned speaker, but I was far from it. Eventually I became that talented, well-seasoned speaker that I pretended to be. I faked it until I was it. In my mind's eye, I saw myself on stage speaking to huge crowds. I studied other great speakers. I hired several speaking coaches. I attended every speaking seminar I could find. Each year I would travel to attend the

Toastmaster International World Championship of Public Speaking. I wanted to surround myself with other people who were doing exactly what I chose to do with the rest of my life. I ordered professional business cards with the words, "Motivational Speaker" in large letters across top of each card. I passed them out to everyone I came in contact with. I didn't introduce myself as SaBrina Fisher Reece, an "aspiring motivational speaker." I proudly greeted them saying "My name is SaBrina Fisher Reece, I am a motivational speaker." Believe in the unseen, act as if you already are exactly who you want to be. Fake it until you feel it and it will become a reality.

Throughout my journey of transformation if ever there was a time that I became discouraged and I was entertaining negative thoughts, I would pick up a book or watch a video by one of our legendary thought leaders. I have read so many books that date as far back as the very early 1900's. Some of my favorite influencers that seem to think very similar to me are: William Walker Atkinson, Eckhart Tolle, Don Miguel Ruiz, Norman Vincent Peale, Greg Braden, Earnest Holmes, Earl Nightingale, Zig Ziglar, W. Clement Stone, Marianne Williamson, Edgar Casey, Joseph Murphy, Nevelle Goodard, Ralph Waldo Emerson, Frederick J. Eikerenkoetter II (Rev. Ike), Joseph Murphy, Robert Collier, and many more. I trained myself to engulf myself in positive thinking whenever I would find myself returning to an old way of thinking. Doing this truly helps it to become a habitual practice. It can take years to retrain our brains and undo all of the negative programming we have lived with most of our lives, but it's vital that we all do it if we sincerely want to have a happy productive life.

The Will

There is something in each of us called, "The Will." The Will is that powerful driving force within us all that gives us the strength and determination to go after what we want. At times it may appear that others have a stronger will than we do. However, we can crank that inner knob on our own "Will" and turn it up to full speed at any point. William Walker Atkinson says, "The Will is the outward manifestation of the 'I Am.'" I completely agree. "I Am" is the most powerful phrase we can say. It leaves no room for future hope and wishes. The statement "I Am," represents now! It represents being completely in the current moment, not believing in or waiting for something to happen later but accepting it as already existing now. Understand the difference between being hopeful for something we desire in the future and claiming that thing to already exist in the present. Even if you can't see or touch it yet, fake it! Feel it! Express gratitude for it now. Act as if it is already there. If you are sad, act happy. If you are poor, act rich. Fake it until you actually feel it and it will soon materialize.

Many people have survived devastating circumstances because they had the will to live. We don't have to wait for a life or death situation to invoke our will. We are the fuel that powers up the Will. When we decide to go full force after our dreams, we find that we are stronger, smarter, and more driven than we could have ever imagined.

Your mind is a gift, open it!
-SaBrina Fisher Reece

Chapter 6

It's All Possible

All things are possible, and I know it's hard for us to believe that at times, especially when everything in our lives seems to be going wrong and all of what we desire hasn't shown up. Times when that home loan was denied, or our relationship seems to be falling apart. Maybe we have lost our job, or our car has been repossessed. It seems that none of our prayers have been answered. These are the times when it's hardest to believe that all things are possible, but they are.

It is during these times when we feel defeated that we allow our vibration to become low. We are all energy and we are all vibrating. We appear to be solid, as do the chair we sit in or the car we drive, but everything is vibrating. You can't see it, but you are vibrating at this very moment. What most don't know is that they can change the frequency of their personal vibration. We can choose to vibrate at a higher frequency. It seems natural that during the hardest times of our lives, when tragedy strikes us or our families, or when finances are low and no ends seem to meet, that we feel stressed and afraid. Acknowledge those feelings, but don't stay there. No matter what you are going through, you still have to encourage yourself and raise your vibration.

I became inspired once I realized that I could change the way I felt. I never had to accept being in a bad mood, no matter what I believed the cause of it to be. If by chance I woke up feeling down, learning that I did not have to accept those feelings and carry them throughout my day was very helpful. We all have the opportunity to reject negative feelings as soon as we recognize them and use whichever tool we find effective in making ourselves instantly feel better. Gospel music or listening to 432 hz binaural beats works well for me. The gospel music instantly makes me happy and grateful. The pure tone version of the 432 hz binaural beats helps me to concentrate, especially when writing. Find what works for you and don't hesitate to use it to center yourself and to uplift your mood.

A quick way for me to pull myself out of a negative space is to write down and acknowledge the things I have to be grateful for. We all have many things to be grateful for. If you are having money problems, but you still have a job, then you have something to be grateful for. If your car isn't running at its best but it's still running and getting you to that job every day, then you have something to be grateful for. If you are employed, allow yourself to feel gratitude for having a job when many do not. Simply taking a moment to sit with and bask in those feelings of gratitude will instantly encourage you. Feeling encouraged motivates us to accomplish more in life.

It is imperative that we realize it takes a conscious effort to make positive change on a subconscious level. If we want a better, more productive life, especially internally, then we must take external steps towards securing our internal happiness. We must come to understand that the internal is just as important or even more important than the external. We must work daily on the subjective aspect of happiness in order to reap the objective benefits of a great life. Subjective things are things you cannot see, feel or touch. Objective things are tangible, things we can touch and see. If we master subjective/internal happiness, objective/external happiness is soon to follow.

Like attracts like. Positive attracts positive and negative attracts negative. It is an immutable universal law. Just like gravity and karma. No matter what you do or who you are if you jump off the roof of a building you will go down. The results of karma are not as visible, but they are unchangeable as well. Kindness returns unto you kindness, hate returns hate it's unavoidable. Universal laws are laws that are inflexible and not subject to change. They are the laws of God.

The Law of Attraction is definitely something you should familiarize yourself with. You attract back to you exactly the energy and vibration that you put out into the world. If you get up in the morning and you aren't feeling your best, take a few minutes before you get up to raise your vibration. Intentionally uplift the way you feel inside so the energy you release into the world is positive. Don't allow yourself to stay in a bad mood or stay sad, unhappy, or disappointed. Low energy attracts more low energy. High energy does the same. We can't afford to proceed with the tasks of our day without elevating our energetic frequency. If you want to have a great day, take a few moments and first speak that intent into the universe. Actually, say the words "Today will be a great day." Better yet, say, "Today Is a great day." Speak of it as a fact and not a wish. Repeat that while you brush your teeth and do your other morning rituals. What most people aren't aware of is that words and thoughts have an energetic frequency too. When you speak negatively, saying things such as, "I'm broke," "I'm dumb," or "I will never get ahead in life," you project that negativity into the world. What you send out comes back. Let's work on making sure the things that come back are good and positive.

We are subconsciously programmed to instantly put up barriers to impede our own thoughts of greatness and success. Try to monitor your thoughts enough to catch yourself the next time it happens. Eventually it will become a positive habit that will change your life.

I used to say to myself, "I want to own a laundromat," but no sooner than the thought came into my mind, I would have thoughts which said, "No, that's too much work," or "Where would you find all those washing machines? You know nothing about this type of business SaBrina." These are self-sabotaging thoughts. This is an example of how we talk ourselves out of greatness. These are the barriers I am speaking of. We create these untruths in our minds. It is for us to simply plant the seed in the garden and allow it to grow. Plant a positive seed not a negative one. We need not concern ourselves with the particulars of how it will be manifested, we just need to believe wholeheartedly that it will. We absolutely must "believe in things unseen as if they already are"

"Now Faith is the substance of things hoped for, the evidence of things unseen." (Hebrew 11:1)

This may not always be the easiest thing to do, but it's the key to being able to manifest your heart's desires into your life. Pretend! Pretend as a child would. Pretend you have that home you want; pretend you have already opened that business you have been dreaming about. Commit an extensive amount of time thinking about it. Literally close your eyes and see the big "Grand Opening" sign in your mind. Design the lettering and the colors. Visualize the people coming in the front door with big smiles congratulating you on the opening day of your business. Force yourself to smile and allow yourself to fill up inside with pride for your accomplishment. Stick with that visual long enough to actually feel the corresponding emotion at that moment. Keep the images in your head until you can connect emotions with them as well. The visual Image plus emotion is key. You'll know it's working when you find yourself smiling externally and internally.

I can always tell when I am following my destined path. People will show up in my life and strike up a conversation that mirrors my own concepts and beliefs. This positive thinking ideology is not always well-received. Many times, I am hesitant to bring up the way I think to others. Even as I type this, I know that despite a huge percentage of the world not being open enough to hear and accept that we are in control of our destiny, and that our thoughts and feelings shape that very destiny, I know that my purpose here on this earth is to continue to deliver that message. Part of my mission here on Earth is to teach people the tools I used to transform my mindset, which ultimately transformed my entire life.

When I come across an author, thought, leader, or speaker who seems to be on the same path I'm on, it makes me emotional. Positive emotions flood through me because even if those people never know I read their book, or watched their videos, my life was impacted by their work because they followed their purpose. My goal is to do the same for others with my literary work. My books and speeches will impact lives. That is what motivates me to continue. The fact that others will learn to love themselves and live their lives to the fullest makes it all worth it.

All things are possible. See yourself in your mind's eye exactly as the person you want to be. You can be anyone you truly want to be. In no way am I insinuating that developing intentional positive pictures in your head is easy. It takes work and a lot of practice. However, this will be the best skill you've ever learned. Mastering this skill will allow you to take part in all the wonderful things this world has to offer.

The practice of creative visualization will get easier and easier. You can hone this skill by attempting to visualize small things like a banana. Close your eyes and tell your mind you see a banana, then switch it to an apple. Learning to creatively visualize takes practice. The images may seem fuzzy or unclear at first. As you continue to do it you will see how quickly the images you call upon appear faster and faster the more you practice this technique. Eventually the images will be clear and solid. You will see how the mind creates pictures instantly as soon as we think of them. That's how God and the universe work. Plant the image with your thoughts and let God do the rest. Remember mastering this ability takes focused intentional time and practice just like any other skill. Please don't get frustrated and quit. Sticking with this will change your life as it did mine. This is the amazing magic of your mind.

We no longer have to live in a world where we have to sacrifice some of our desires for others. Everything is a possibility; we simply have to learn how to bring them to us. We don't have to give up on wealth to have happiness, or sacrifice the desire for peace in order to be successful. We can have it all.

I don't know anyone who does not want more of something in life, be it peace of mind, abundant wealth, or happiness. Everyone has hopes and dreams of something more. This book will reinforce the fact that you can indeed have exactly what you want and plenty of it. However, many people are unsure of exactly what they desire. What do you want? What will make you happy? Sit down and clarify in detail precisely what you believe needs to be added to your life to make you pleased and content. Our thoughts escape us at times. We will think or dream of something and after proceeding with our daily activities we will forget. I suggest always keeping a journal with you to jot down your thoughts, goals and ideas as quickly as your mind delivers them to you. Many of those ideas will prove to be quite valuable. Later, you can pick one at a time and visualize having it. Give each thing you list in your journal its own individual creative visualization time. Practice this positive tool daily and soon it will astonish you how fast all of the wonderful things show up in your life.

Remember, all things are possible; not some, but all. I repeat that continuously because I want you to know that there is no goal that is too big. It's all possible! Accepting that is one of the first steps in changing your life through positive thinking. There are no limits other than the ones we accept in our mind. We must learn how to maintain a positive state of mind, because doing so will drastically change the things that show up in our lives. Remember that the mind is our own personal garden. It accepts exactly what we plant. It's our genie in a bottle. The mind will grant our true wishes, good or bad. We must understand that. The mind won't say, "No, I don't think that is a good idea." If you plant it, it will grow!

Everything you desire is possible, bad things included. We must not focus on bad thoughts. We have the ability to manifest undesirable things into our lives also. Things that are not in our best interest or in line with God's plan for us are also possible. All things are possible, so we must guide our thoughts toward the possibilities we sincerely want in our lives.

Do not waste time thinking and fearing that you will have a car accident, or you will. Do not focus your mind power on your fears of divorce or that is the very thing that will happen to your marriage. The thoughts we allow our minds to concentrate on will show up in our actual lives. Many of us do not realize how much time we spend thinking of the things we fear.

What you fear will appear! You can be certain of that. Take time to identify what those fears are so you can recognize them when they show up in your mind and quickly eliminate them.

Once we fully understand that anything we apply focused thought to can and will appear in our lives, then we should not continue to resist the fact that it's necessary to learn to focus on the good and positive, and cast out all other thoughts before they materialize. Many of the things present in my life today, I have to admit, I committed a significant amount of time thinking of them. Good or bad, the rules are the same. Catch yourself the next time you find yourself daydreaming. It may seem harmless, but once you stop yourself and immediately reflect back to what you were just daydreaming about, you may find it was not positive. If that is the case, then you will see why this practice is necessary. Catch those negative, fearful thoughts immediately and switch them into positive ones.

The Bible states in Matthew 19:26, "But Jesus Beheld them and said unto them, "With men this is impossible, but with God all things are possible" or in Luke 1:37 "For with God nothing shall be impossible." Growing up in the Christian church I have heard many different versions of these scriptures combined with their many different interpretations. I believe that from the beginning of time God created us with no limitations. We have always been capable of great, amazing things but somehow we lost our way. At some point in our existence humans seemed to accept restrictions on our lives that were never meant to exist, restrictions that technically do not exist until we convince ourselves that they do. This has been the downfall of mankind. This is why everyone is not a successful inventor, adding their life-changing contributions to the world. We all are capable of great ideas. We are all great. That amazing inspiration for creation is inside of us all. We just need to remember that it's there.

Watching inspirational movies of people who persevered despite great odds and accomplished their dreams are great reminders that we can do anything. Stories such as that of Bart Millard, the lead singer of the group, Mercy Me, have uplifted me. His life story inspired the world in the movie and hit song, "I Can Only Imagine." I've watched this movie at least a dozen times. The feelings of hope that you feel when you watch others strive for success and win are priceless. This is often the push we need to keep going until we accomplish our goals. Knowing that all of our goals are attainable should keep that fire burning in all of us.

Another story that inspired me was the story of Tommy Caldwell and Kevin Jorgeson. They were rock climbers determined to conquer a massive mountain in El Capitan called, "The Dawn Wall." When I began watching the documentary my first thought was, Why would anyone want to do this? Once I finished the show, I realized it does not matter if others understand the "why" as long as we do. Whatever stirs up that drive and gives us the will power needed to recognize that we can do anything is all that matters. For some, it may be climbing the highest mountain. For others, it may be running for president or becoming a best-selling author. Many may have dreams of acting on the big screen or becoming a great singer. Whatever it is that motivates us as humans to keep going, that is what we all need to hold on to.

All goals are attainable. There is no goal you can set for yourself that is too big to accomplish. Do not allow anyone to convince you of that. More importantly, do not convince yourself that certain goals are unattainable. Nothing you desire is insurmountable. If you are willing to commit to the work needed to bring your desires into your reality, then nothing can stop you from achieving them. Yes, the physical work, the hustle and bustle are important, but the most important work is the mental work; learning to keep your thoughts positive. Believe that what you want is already done, not "will be," not "one day," but already done. Close your eyes and feel the feelings of already having what you desire. And like magic you will reap the objective benefits of having it. There is nothing that is impossible. Get a pen and paper, write down your clearly defined goals and get to work.

Abundance Is Real

Abundance is a concept that I speak about regularly. I have several YouTube videos entitled Abundance Is Real. I am very passionate about the fact that I believe all people can experience abundance in all areas of their lives. Financial abundance is something people feel that they have to sacrifice in exchange for good health, happiness, and peace. We do not have to forgo wealth. We can have financial abundance too.

Yes, working hard is half the battle, but I am of the mindset that prosperity begins first in the mind. Your Mind is Magic, and our minds are the magic wand that will allow financial wealth to show up in our lives. The action of work is secondary. One can work all day and night but if he doesn't believe that he deserves abundance he won't have it.

There is a scripture in the bible that says, "For whoever has, he shall be given more, and they will have abundance. Whoever does not have, even what they have will be taken from them". Matthew 13:12

I think many people misinterpret this scripture as God being cruel. That's not it at all. Since poverty is a mindset, God is simply saying for those who believe they deserve wealth will receive more, but for those who gain some degree of financial freedom, but are still of the mindset that they don't deserve it, they will eventually lose it. They will lose it not because they don't deserve it, but because they don't believe that they deserve it. They are surprised by the prosperity, so they expect to lose it. We must train our minds to expect wealth.

Have you ever noticed how some big business tycoons lose everything and go bankrupt, yet somehow rebuild everything in a short amount of time? The only thing they possess that differs from many others is the expectation of success. They see themselves as nothing but wealthy even when their business has failed. Poverty is a mindset that can be changed.

No one has to settle for poverty. The first steps in changing it begins in the mind.

Each one of us is entitled to the riches of the world, but we cannot experience that wealth in its entirety until we rid our minds of a poverty mindset. Understandably, after years of expecting financial hardship it can take a lot of consistent work to reverse those habits. Begin with a simple daily affirmation:

"I am rich in all areas of my life, money flows frequently and effortlessly into my life."

Abundance is real and something we all can enjoy. Make a decision that no matter what your current financial situation, you will begin to thank God daily for abundance. Even if your mind is trying to convince you that you are being dishonest, keep putting thoughts of gratitude out into the universe. Keep telling God, "Thank you," for the wealth he has blessed you with. Act as if you are the wealthiest person in the world. Mentally declare prosperity for yourself and believe me it will appear. Do not try to concern yourself with how and where it will come from. Just believe that is possible and already done.

#AbundanceIsReal

Emancipate yourself from mental slavery, no one but ourselves can free our minds.

-Bob Marley

CHAPTER 7

Close Your Eyes and Visualize

Creative visualization has proven to be so beneficial in my life, which is why I want to share this amazing tool with all of you. I have briefly touched on the subject in the previous chapters, but I want to expand further on it here. We have the power to close our eyes and pretend the things we desire actually exist. Pretending that they exist is the secret to actually manifesting them into your life. Children use their imagination to do this all day long. We are born with this natural ability to create things in our mind. Holding thoughts and images in our minds until we feel as if they are real is the key to bringing all the things we want into our lives. The thoughts we focus on are the ones that matter most. We can control our thoughts, which will give us control over our lives.

Russell Simmons' books, "Super Rich" and "Success Through Stillness," along with Eckhart Tolle's "The Power of Now" were all instrumental in teaching me the importance of sitting still and monitoring my thoughts. "Super Rich" in particular left a great impression on me because being the huge business mogul that Russell is, I'm certain many were drawn to the title believing he was giving the world the secrets of how to attain wealth. I remember how intrigued I was to find that the wealth he spoke of in his book was spiritual and emotional wealth, which are vitally important to sustain financial wealth, but Russell Simmons understood, as I do now, that all the money in the universe won't give you peace of mind.

I get excited about the concepts I speak about in my books and I have unshakable faith in them. However there have been many instances in my life where I had to truly work all the tools I believe in, to recenter myself and return to a place of knowing that what I believe in is indeed real. Life has thrown me many "sucker punches," and during these times I had to reevaluate and reaffirm my beliefs.

I became a grandmother for the first time on June 6, 2019. My oldest daughter, Joi, gave birth to a beautiful baby boy, named Raiden Jesse Spears, named after my father, Jesse Paul

Fisher who died when I was ten. Although my daughter and I tried our best to arrange things so I would not miss Raiden's birth, the minute I got onto a plane headed to Tampa, Florida for a speakers' training with Delatorro McNeal III called "Crush The Stage," she went into labor. I could not believe it. I was beyond devastated. All of our efforts to ensure that the baby came before or after my trip had failed. I could not believe I was going to miss the birth of my first grandchild. I was absolutely inconsolable on the plane. This was not a moment I would ever get back.

I'm still not sure how I was able to receive the message in flight with my cell phone on airplane mode, but somehow it came through while I was still in the air. I was so hurt that I was going to miss this monumental occasion that I began to cry uncontrollably. I got up from my seat and went to the back where three stewardesses were preparing to serve lunch to the passengers. I walked into the back where they were and I just cried and cried to them, telling them I was not going to be present for the birth of my first grandchild. They were very sweet and understanding. They hugged me and gave me a bottle of wine to calm me and I returned to my seat. I still couldn't stop crying. My distress was so loud and obnoxious that I felt obligated to explain to the man sitting next to me what the problem was. He was kind and he said some comforting words, which I don't remember, and I laid my head on the window and attempted to suffer through the remainder of the flight silently.

Approximately one hour before the plane landed I took out one of my journals and began to write a poem for my new grandson:

Baby Raiden
I have waited for you all week Lil' guy
And as soon as I'm up in the sky
You choose to say "Hi",
I have cried like a baby on this plane
The stewardesses thought I was in physical pain.
I told them I'm missing your birth.
They said, "Don't cry - celebrate his journey to earth."
I told them that this was a special time.
They comforted me and gave me free wine.
Grammie can't wait to meet you.
Your life will be so Amazing!
We all love you so much.
I can't wait to meet you and feel your soft new touch
I'm so sorry I'm on a plane headed to train, in another state.

Your Mind is Magic

Trying to make sure that I am Great!
And worthy of the gift of your love.
My precious Grandson, My Lil' Dove.
I will see you soon. I'm filled with Joy.
Welcome to the world Grammie's Baby Boy.

SaBrina Fisher Reece, 6/4/2019

Aside from being absolutely crushed that I missed the birth of my first grandchild, when the plane descended, I felt the most excruciating pain in my ears. I had done a lot of flying over the past four years and never had I experienced anything this uncomfortable. (This was what led to me making an appointment with the ear, nose, and throat specialist, which resulted in the findings mentioned in Chapter 8). The plane landed and I called my daughter from the airport immediately. She was still en route to the hospital to deliver the baby. I sat down inside the airport and she and I cried and cried on the phone like it was the end of the world. We are very close.

I convinced myself that for whatever reason, I was not meant to be there for the delivery. It was the only thought that calmed me. Maybe God didn't feel I would have been able to see her in so much pain. Fortunately, due to modern technology, I was able to view the entire birth via Facetime.

Although I was grateful that I got to see his birth virtually, the stress of the entire situation caused me to be less than prepared for the three-day intensive speakers training that I went to Tampa, Florida to attend. I was distracted, and it took a ton of positive self-talk to get through the training. Each day when I got back to my hotel room, I had to take a moment to close my eyes and visualize myself inside the classroom, speaking confidently on stage. Fortunately, it was a very small class, which made it a lot easier. I learned that at times we may feel we have done all we can to be the best we can, but when we meet others that are better, we realize we need to keep working harder. Our instructor, Delatorro McNeal III, is a world-renowned speaker, and the confidence he exuded onstage was definitely something I wanted for myself. He challenged me in ways that were clearly necessary, but I was intimidated. During my final speech on the third day, he kept stopping me and making me begin again. My ego led me to believe he was picking on me and I began to take it personally. I know better than to take things personally, but in these moments, I could not fight it off. There was a moment where I had a choice: to sit down, get my feelings in check and return to the stage and deliver my speech again, or walk out. Since walking out is not my style and goes against everything I believe in, I sat down and got my nerves together first, then I began to write affirmations on postcards reassuring myself that I could do this.

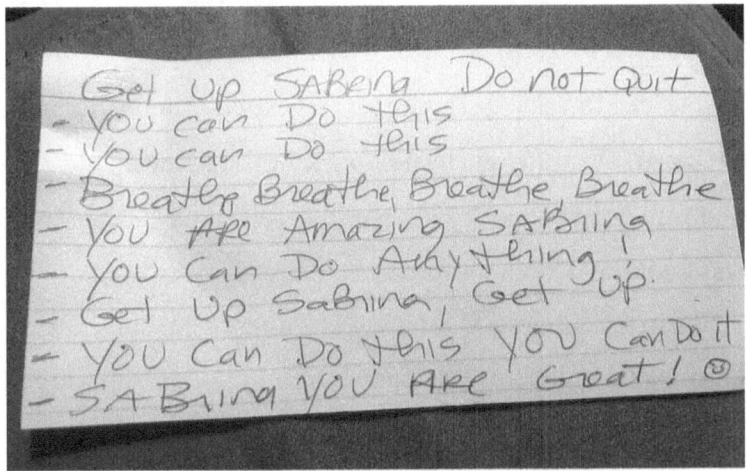

I was scared to death to go back on stage and possibly be stopped mid-speech again, but something inside me knew that if I could get through this, I would be a much better speaker in the end. My heart was pounding. I tried in those few moments to script something, but I knew it was best If I simply spoke from my heart. Other than the instructor and students, several other people had been invited to judge and evaluate our final presentations. That additional pressure definitely didn't make it easier. My old friend, "Ego", crept into my mind while I was waiting to go back up again and tried to convince me that the evaluations from the instructor and the guest were biased. "They didn't like me," is what I attempted to tell myself. I wanted to run with that, but one thing I'm excellent at is recognizing ego. Ego is no friend to us and it will distract us from completing tasks we need to evolve to the next level. I traveled to Tampa for this expert training because after years of studying Delatorro McNeal, I knew he was the best, so I quickly told "ego" to shut up and move the heck on, and I continued to breathe and encourage myself.

I got up after restructuring my speech in only fifteen minutes in my head. My nerves were at an all-time high, but mentally I was determined to incorporate some of the techniques that were given to me after my first evaluation. This was one of the hardest things I have ever done. I had to do a lot of self-talk, but I was there to learn. I had to lay my ego down and become completely humble. I felt attacked. I was very emotional and felt like a failure, however it was all in my mind. Not one of the judges called me a failure or said any of those negative things I was thinking to me. I said them to myself in my mind. I had to work through that, and I had to do it quickly. I wanted to scream, walk out, and give up but I knew I would never forgive myself, nor would I learn the lesson that the universe used this moment to teach me. I took several deep breaths and cast away the negative thoughts. I continued my internal affirmations all the way back to the stage.

Needless to say, I did it! I landed it within the allotted ten minutes given to each student. I delivered a magnificent speech, implementing all of the new tools I just learned which earned me my "Crush The Stage" speaking certificate. It helped me advance greatly as a speaker. I learned so much from that experience. I grew in so many areas. I pushed myself when I truly was so emotional from the initial critique that I wanted to give up. I learned to incorporate techniques into my speech that would allow me to humbly sell my book from the stage as well. Selling from the stage is unquestionably something I had no idea how to do. I had been giving my book away because I wanted others to have the skills I used to feel better in life. Most importantly I tested the very tools I teach to others on myself, and they worked! I needed to encourage myself in that uncomfortable moment and I did. Although I thought I was going to die at the time, I am so glad I stuck it out and I would do it all over again.

When I got back to my hotel room to decompress from it all I was so sincerely proud of myself. I utilized the very tools of affirmations and creative visualization to make myself get back on that stage when every ounce of me wanted to quit. I did not quit, and I left there feeling great. Internal work is not always easy, but the mental battles are the very ones we need to win. Going to full-out war with the internal enemies of ego, self-doubt and fear will prove to be the most significant war you will ever fight. I may have missed the birth of my grandson, but I developed something so wonderful with-in myself that made it all worth it. I returned home the next day to meet my beautiful first grandchild.

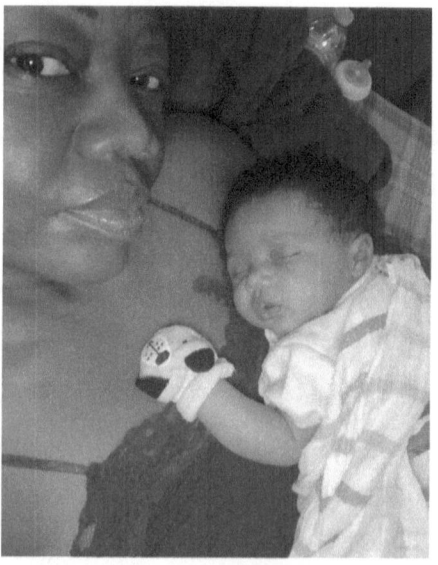

I am so grateful to have lived long enough to see my children's children. There were many times throughout my life that I never thought I would live long enough to see my grandchildren, but once I took control of my life and began to use my natural gift of imagination to create a better life, I became excited about living. I became even more excited about creating a great life. I no longer believe that I was doomed to suffer throughout this life experience as I once did. I began working on changing the narrative in my head. I wanted to live a long healthy life, but I knew I had to mentally create that reality. I had to reprogram all of the images of death. I would practice seeing myself at a much older age. I would create images of having conversations with my great-grandchildren, embracing and encouraging them in full mind, body, and soul. We don't just want to live a long life, we must do the mental work to ensure a long, healthy life, free of sickness and disease. No one is meant to simply suffer through life. We are all meant to be happy. Happiness begins inside first. Imagine that you are happy, healthy and prosperous and before you know it you will be.

Training your imagination is not easy, start with simple exercises. Imagine yourself five years from now walking into the home you desire to live in. Imagine the car you want to drive. Imagine the beautiful grass and flowers outside of your new home. If you have a fear of death, imagine yourself at a much later stage in life signifying that you will live a long life.

When I get fearful of death, I imagine myself at my eighty-fifth birthday party. I imagine myself smiling and dancing and basking in the joy of being surrounded by all of my children, grandchildren and great-grandchildren. I make sure to be specific in the visual by seeing myself strong and healthy enjoying my birthday. That part is very important. We must be detailed when we do our visualization techniques. You wouldn't want to create a scene where you live to be one hundred but you are sick, disabled, and unhealthy would you? Make sure you visualize yourself happy and healthy. God gave us the power to think anything we desire into existence. This power is active even when we are not aware of it. That is why monitoring our thoughts is necessary.

I have owned several businesses, some of which I knew nothing about before opening. Inked 4 Life Tattoo Studio is proof that you can precisely design something completely in your mind before it exists in the real world. I initially took possession of a commercial building because I created a barber shop for my son Justin who was in barber school. I named that salon, "Just-In-Time Barber and Beauty Salon." After spending an enormous amount of time and money putting this business together it became apparent that my son did not want the responsibility of being a business owner. He said he wanted to become a rapper, which was the dream of so many young African American boys at the time. I always told him that he did not have to continue this as a lifelong career, but it would give him a source of income until he figured out exactly what he wanted to be.

Justin was quite strong-willed, and I was stuck with a barber shop that I had no desire or time to run. I always let my son know that he did not have to make a career out of the barber shop. It was simply my gift to him to generate an income until he was able to pursue his dreams. However he was still quite disinterested in running it. My primary business, Braids By SaBrina, was located two doors down, and it consumed the majority of my time and energy. However, I was locked into a lease for a few years, so I needed to do something with the building. I drove around and scanned the neighborhood for ideas of what I could transform the barber-shop into. I came up with the idea of a tattoo shop. Tattooing was quite popular and there was no direct competitor anywhere near. I knew nothing of how to run this particular type of business. My only experience with tattoo shops was when I had gone to one to receive a tattoo. However, in my mind I began to create the business. This was at a time in my life where I had no idea the importance of creative visualization. I had not yet learned these mental tools, but by default I designed this business in my mind from beginning to end. It had beautiful, fluorescent green lettering to catch the attention of those in oncoming traffic. Fortunately, I was able to utilize most of the furniture from the barber shop. I did a lot of the artwork on the wall myself. I even drew a large koi fish on the floor. It was a fun and exciting new experience.

In my sleep, I would come up with ideas and then get up and implement them the next day. I repeat I had no experience whatsoever in the tattoo industry. I went around town and visited other tattoo parlors to get an idea of the basic setup. Thirty days later I opened the doors to Inked 4 Life Tattoo Studio on Adams Blvd. A full- fledged business that began as a simple thought.

Your Mind is Magic

Our minds are so amazing. The mind is indeed magical. Even before I knew how to use visualization techniques as a tool, I was successful in using them by default. When I think back on how I used my mind to create that business, I get inspired. I never allowed fear or doubt to enter my mind. I never once remember thinking that it was not possible to own a tattoo shop. I visualized it and voila! I became the sole proprietor of yet another successful business. That opportunity exists for everyone. Thinking back on that reminds me that we can do absolutely anything as long as we ignore those little voices in our heads that tell us we cannot.

We are creators and anything we truly desire we can have. I believe this should be taught in kindergarten. Children should learn, as early as possible of the power they possess over their own lives. They should be taught that their lives are like a coloring book and only they possess the crayons. I believe that mankind can indeed evolve, but it starts with each and every individual person recognizing their own greatness. We all must come to terms with the fact that we are not limited unless we choose to be. We can become anyone we chose to become. The possibilities are limitless. We can acquire any level of success we choose. We simply have to train our minds to believe that all things are possible.

@In59Seconds

Master your mind and all will fall in line.
-SaBrina Fisher Reece

CHAPTER 8

Unexpected Journey

It was a warm Sunday afternoon in 2012. I was enjoying the company of my oldest daughter Joi, who was seventeen years old at the time and a twelfth grade student at St. Mary's Academy (Blue Tie). She and I always had a great relationship. On this day she and I were walking around the track at Norman O. Houston park, not far from our home and I suddenly got a debilitating cramp in my lower abdomen. My daughter was instantly frightened and concerned. She asked, "Mom are you okay?" I couldn't answer because I was trying to breathe and allow the cramps to subside.

Once it passed, she and I gave each other an odd look and continued walking around the track. I hadn't been feeling my best, so I was attempting to return to a regular workout regimen because according to Google, the symptoms I had been experiencing were very similar to diabetes. I had been experiencing severe nausea, blurred vision, and frequent trips to the bathroom. My biological mother was an insulin-dependent diabetic, so I was afraid that genetics had caught up with me. I figured if that was the case, I should get a head start on the disease before I went to the doctor for an official diagnosis.

We continued walking when my daughter asked, "Mom do you think there is any chance you may be pregnant?" I looked at her and laughed hysterically. I said, "Baby, I am forty-two years old. I have given birth to three children. Don't you think I would know my body well enough that if I were pregnant, I would definitely know? Furthermore, what do you know about pregnancy anyway?" We laughed and continued exercising.

The thought of pregnancy wasn't even realistic in my mind. I had reached an age where things in women become inconsistent, I was past the age where one even considers pregnancy, and I was working out and getting my mind and body ready for my self-diagnosed diabetes, which I was certain I had inherited from my biological mother.

Eventually, my symptoms got so bad that I went to the emergency room at Gardena Memorial Hospital. Once I was brought into the nurse, she asked the standard question "What brings you here today?" I replied, "I already know what's wrong, diabetes runs in my family and I'm just about positive I have it." I pulled out a list that I had brought with me of all the facts and symptoms about diabetes that I had gotten off the internet. I showed the list to her and she gave me a strange look.

She then asked, "Ms. Reece, is there any chance you could be pregnant?" I said, "No, no ma'am, I'm forty-two years old, those days are long gone for me."

She said, "Well, Ms. Ole' Lady, we still have to do a standard pregnancy test."

I agreed, but I told her it was a complete waste of time because I was too old to be pregnant. My youngest child was 11 at the time and I hadn't had a normal menstrual cycle in years.

They proceeded with the test, but the emergency room was extremely crowded, so it took hours. I had also convinced them that I could possibly have gallstones because I did feel something weird in my stomach. Just as they were going to send me upstairs to have an ultrasound to look for gallstones or other causes for pain in my stomach, a nurse came in and said, "Ms. Reece..." By that time, I was lying down, attempting to sleep. I sat up and said, "Yes?" She said, "Ms. Reece, you're pregnant!"

Time stood still. My brain began to race, I replied, "No, I'm not! That's precisely why I'm here, because I'm not pregnant, but I have all these symptoms." She looked at me and realized I wasn't prepared to receive what she was saying, so she turned around and walked out of the room. About ten minutes later, she returned with the doctor and another nurse with the positive pregnancy test in hand. Once again, she said, "Ms. Reece, you are pregnant!"

I could not believe my ears. I began to sweat, and my mind began to race. I immediately started thinking about a glass of wine I had with dinner. Pregnant at forty-two. No way. I was in shock. The ultrasound that had been scheduled to search for gallstones was then changed, and I was sent upstairs to see the newfound fetus. Much to my surprise, I was not only definitely pregnant, I was 14 weeks pregnant. This was April 18, 2012.

I celebrated my 43rd Birthday on August 7, 2012 while on bed rest and exactly six months from the day I found out about her, on October 18, 2012, a beautiful healthy baby girl whom I named Journey Schy Morris made her unexpected journey into the world and into our hearts.

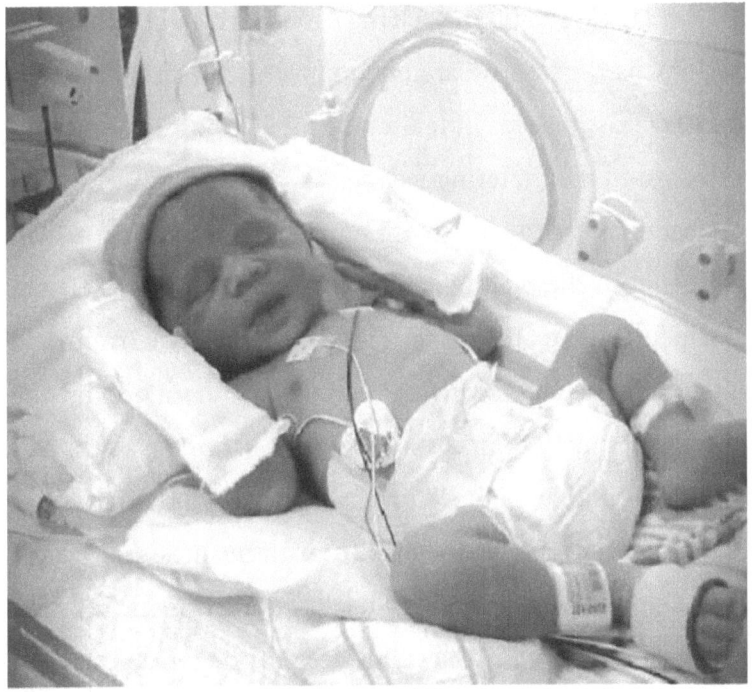

Journey Schy Morris, born October 18, 2012

I told this story because I want you to realize how strong subconscious beliefs can be. I sincerely believed that I had diabetes and that belief existed because of my knowledge of my biological mother having this illness. I believed that it was my genetic destiny to develop the same disease. When instead there was a beautiful blessing growing inside of me.

Let's try hard not to block the Amazing blessings that God had for us because we are uncompromisable in our beliefs. It's very possible this little life was moving inside of me, but I dismissed the fluttering feelings as something else because my belief in eventually becoming diabetic was stronger than my belief in the possibility of naturally becoming pregnant at age forty-two. Our subconscious beliefs can be strong and unshakable which is why we must attack them one by one and dissect them to make sure they are serving us well. Our beliefs need to be in line with exactly what we desire for our lives. You can't say you want to start a business but have a secret hidden belief that you will fail at that business. You can't say you desire a loving mate but deep inside of you there is a belief that you will never find a good mate. The deep-rooted subconscious belief will win every time.

God's plan for us may be perfect health but we "Believe" we are supposed to suffer from sickness and disease because our past relatives did. Therefore, because of the free will the Creator gave us to design our own lives, despite God's plan for great health for us, disease shows up instead. Many of us are taught by our parents and grandparents that we are doomed to develop the diseases of our ancestors and I clearly believed that for many years. I no longer share that belief. Despite the fact that certain genetic markers may be present, I no longer believe that we are genetically predisposed to disease. I know now that God gave all human beings the ability to transcend those apparent genetic sick genes with our minds. Your mind is magic!

The mind is amazingly powerful. It is so powerful, that although I had symptoms of pregnancy, I ignored them because of my subconscious programming. Baby Journey was growing inside of me, yet my mind had convinced me of something completely different. Even when I felt typical pregnancy symptoms like fatigue, frequent urination, and nausea, I ignored them and diagnosed myself with something else that was easier to believe in. Remember the bible says, "It is done unto you as you believe." So, recognizing what our true beliefs are is vital. The things that show up in your life are based solely off of your belief system. Take some time to figure out exactly what you believe.

Mind is all. We must identify what we truly believe. I no longer believe in the possibilities of long term sickness and disease. I reinforce that with daily affirmations by saying,

"Sickness and disease do not live in my body."

"I am healthy and wealthy in all areas of my life."

Perfect health is a concept that I want everyone in the world to adopt. Mentally embrace the concept of perfect health. Even when physical ailments are present. View them as temporary, just passing through your body, possibly to slow us down and bring awareness to something God wants us to pay attention to, but do not mentally accept them as permanent.

Studying the placebo effect helped me to confirm my belief that sickness is optional. I am definitely not asking anyone to stop taking your prescribed medication or ignore advice given by your doctor. I am merely suggesting that you take your medicine and follow the physician's orders with an optimistic mindset. Believing that you are already healed.

Make no mistake, although I sincerely do not believe that sickness and disease have to be a deathly fate for anyone or even a physically debilitating one. There still seems to be times when unfortunate physical situations happen no matter how evolved we believe ourselves to be. Several times throughout my forties, I experienced high blood pressure and had to be put on medication. I was so against it that I removed myself from it for two years and replaced the medicine with exercise, ginger root and apple cider vinegar. I would never be irresponsible or suggest to anyone to stop taking their medication. I do believe it was my strong belief in the alternative measures that

I was taking that allowed me to be successful in staying off medicine for two years and not having any complications. I honestly understand why medical doctors warn about genetic predisposition to illness, however it is my strong opinion that despite genetic markers and despite statistics, the Mind has the ability to transcend all sickness and disease. Take your medication but take it with the belief that whatever physical ailment you are experiencing is temporary and simply passes through your body on its way out.

How grateful I was that I had spent years strengthening that belief in perfect health. In late 2019, after waking up from a surgery to remove my tonsils, adenoids and re-open my eardrum, I was told that when going into my ear to drain what they believed to be a cyst with the hopes of re-opening my eardrum and restoring the 30% hearing loss that I was experiencing in my left ear, that what they thought was a harmless cyst was actually a tumor and would require brain surgery to remove.

Initially, despite my daily attempts to remain positive, I was disappointed that someone who completely rejects the idea of sickness could receive a diagnosis like this.

Acoustic Neuroma; a benign tumor that sits on the hearing and facial nerves in the brain. I was told my tumor had also wrapped itself around my facial nerves, so removing it could cause partial facial paralysis. The idea of that was very unsettling. I was afraid.

Sometimes you want to scream and ask God, "Why isn't my life perfect?"

Why weren't my affirmations working? I was no different than other people who became doubtful and afraid, but the only significant difference was that I knew the danger of staying in that place. I remember being sad and having a "Why me?" pity party. I even made a video about it, but soon after, I quickly started allowing the gratitude to change my attitude. I was grateful that the tumor was not only found, but most importantly, not cancerous. Once I began to focus on the positive in the situation, I felt much better. Shortly after my initial surgery and diagnosis, I traveled to Istanbul, Turkey, and Athens, Delphi, Meteora and Santorini, Greece, and I had a magnificent time.

I had a few friends that begged me not to go due to their fear of the pressure of flying affecting the tumor, but I was not going to live or think in fear. Not only did I go on the wonderful trip, I didn't experience the pain during the flight that my doctor told me to expect. I enjoyed all of these beautiful cities with women that I have grown to love dearly. Many of whom I have also traveled with to Indonesia, Peru, and Egypt. These women have become my family. We all still keep in touch and continue to cultivate our positive relationships currently. I love them all dearly.

Athens Greece. November 2019

When I returned home from my trip, I made an appointment with the neurosurgeon and moved forward with a hopeful, more positive attitude.

I began to focus on my belief in sound healing and spent a lot of time meditating to specific sounds such as 432 and 528 megahertz binary tones. I bought a key of #A pineal sound bowl, which I absolutely love, and a tuning fork. I set an intention to visualize the tumor shrinking each time I used the sound bowl and fork.

Belief is Everything when you make a choice to create and implement positive practices in your life it is vital that you believe wholeheartedly in them. On my second visit to the neurosurgeon after careful study of my MRI images. Dr. Sean Xin confirmed that no brain surgery is needed. He said the location of the tumor is slightly outside of the brain, which will require only a simple, noninvasive, less critical surgery that can be done by an ear, nose, and throat specialist.

Although the concept of self-healing is new to me, I believe in it strongly. I believe God gave us everything we need on this earth to nourish and heal our own bodies. The ancestors before us knew the healing properties of this amazing planet. I'm excited about learning more about natural herbs and how they benefit the human body, but what I'm certain of is the trust in nature's remedies must still be coupled with the strong mental belief in them.

Do I believe that my thought process coupled with my daily positive habitual practices are responsible for the outcome of my medical situation? Absolutely! God gave us the amazing power to create an image in our minds of perfection.

We have been equipped with all the tools we need to design a magnificent life, free of illness. I will spend the rest of my life mastering these tools and teaching others to do the same.

There have been a few other times in my life where I felt God's amazing divine energy intervened on my behalf. When I began branding myself as a motivational speaker, I would make sure to attend every seminar that came to town. Les Brown, whom I have studied extensively from the time I decided I wanted to speak, was in Los Angeles for an empowerment seminar called, "Get Motivated." I couldn't wait to attend the event. A couple of my Toastmasters friends were going as well. We weren't able to get seats in the front, which would have been my preference, but we all happily settled in on row 17. There were many speakers that came on before Les Brown, but I was patiently awaiting his arrival. He was my inspiration. I am certain I had seen every single motivational video he had made, and I was honored to see him speak in person.

Hours went by and suddenly I saw an old friend of mine walking down the center aisle. I got up to speak to her and she was just as thrilled to see me as I was her. We hugged and I briefly told her that I was a motivational speaker now. She asked where I was sitting. I pointed to the seventeenth row.

She said, "Girl, I'm bringing you to the front with me." I told her I had a couple of friends with me. She eventually moved all my friends to the second and third rows as well. When it was time for Les Brown to come out, she literally had someone take a chair and place it in the front row directly in front of Les Brown center stage. I could not believe it. There I was, seated directly in front of the man whose words aided in my mental and spiritual transformation over the past few years. It was as if God said, "You are great, let Me place you in the seat of greatness." I recognized the blessing instantly. I was so grateful for my friends' efforts. I later asked her, "Did you know I was an aspiring motivational speaker before today?" She said she had no clue. She had never seen my motivational YouTube videos. God uses people, places, and things to make our dreams come true. Divine intervention at its finest took place that day. I was completely OK with being in the back. I was just happy to be there, but God said, "Nope, this is my gift to you," which made me feel like I was definitely on the correct path for my life. I sat filled with gratitude and thrilled by the confirmation that God will grant you the desires of your heart. That day, July 29, 2015, I was a true recipient of God's favor, without a doubt. I have never doubted that I would be a famous, life changing motivational and inspirational speaker one day, but it sure feels good when the universe conspires to grant you your heart's desires.

SaBrina sitting in front of Les Brown

I recognized this immediately as manifestation. On this day, in that room was exactly where I was supposed to be. I knew I had called this moment into existence with my thoughts. On so many occasions I had thought of meeting Les Brown and now here I was in a seat made just for me staring up at the famous Les Brown.

The Number 33

My oldest daughter has always believed in numerology. I wasn't a non-believer, but I simply had not given it much thought. I live in South Los Angeles, where the popular rapper,

Nipsey Hussle owned a store called "The Marathon." His store was located within walking distance from my home. There was a burger place located in the same shopping center of his store, but I rarely went there because there were always a lot of guys hanging out. Unfortunately, in 2019, Nipsey was shot and killed directly in front of his place of business. This outraged the community and there was an abundance of neighborhood support.

While the world was watching his widely televised funeral I chose not to initially. I always wake up in the early morning somewhere between 3:00 and 4:00 am. One morning shortly after 3:00 AM, as usual I woke up and for some strange reason, I logged onto my YouTube and began finally watching what the majority of the world had already seen a few days prior. While watching the funeral video, I discovered that Nipsey had died at age thirty-three. Since his death I noticed him frequently being compared to Jesus Christ, who had also been killed at age thirty-three. I remember thinking how unusual that was. I continued watching the funeral footage. While doing so I began to receive notifications to my personal YouTube channel. I clicked the notifications and many of them were comments from people who had viewed a video of mine that had been posted approximately two years prior. The title of the video is "Motivational Speaker SaBrina Fisher Reece speaking at KRST Unity Center of Afrakan Spiritual Science." I clicked onto my video and my eyes were immediately drawn to the "likes." It had been liked thirty-three times. The notifications were comments all saying things like, "Nipsey Hussle's mother sent me here." Nipsey's mother was a member of KRST, and had mentioned the Unity Center during the funeral.

I went to wake up my daughter because I knew she would find these numerical similarities interesting, and as I handed her my phone, I noticed that my battery life read 33%. I looked at her in disbelief. I said "There is no way this is all coincidence. She found it intriguing and when she woke up that morning, she researched the number 33 and texted it to me. When I received her text it was 7:33am.

I became an instant believer in numerology. After studying and researching the number 33 we found that it is known to be a Master Number, and resonates with the energies of compassion, blessings, inspiration, honesty, discipline, bravery and courage. According to several experts in this field, the number 33 tells us that 'all things are possible.' It is said that the number 33 is also the number that symbolizes guidance. I am not exactly sure what I believe the connection to be, but I am certain that on that particular day I was meant to acknowledge the connection. I have my own interpretation of why it happened. It could be as simple as the universe letting me know that I am on the correct spiritual path. Perception is relative, but I choose to believe that God was attempting to deliver a message. I believe the message was simply confirming that I am on the right spiritual path.

At the very least, it opened my mind to the possibility that everything is connected. I can only assume that as I continue to grow spiritually the numerical, spiritual, geometric, astrological and other connections will all become clear to me. I'm looking forward to connecting all the dots.

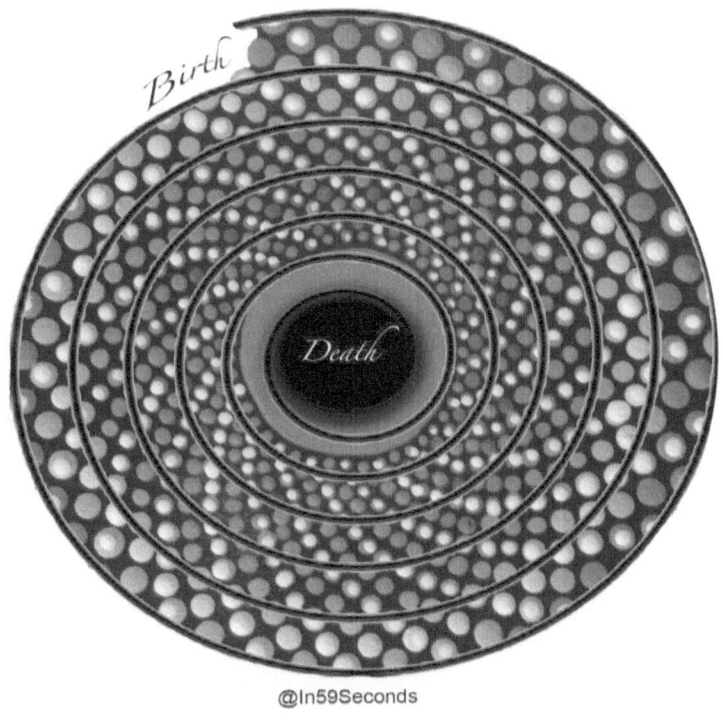

To the mind that is still, the whole universe surrenders.
- Lao Tzu

Chapter 9

Recognize Reject Replace

The one proven tool that has worked wonders for me when it comes to eliminating my mind of a negative thinking pattern is catching the thought as it is coming in and making a conscious choice to cast it right back out. We can't change a negative thinking pattern if we have not first recognized that it is present. We must take some time to notice each and every thought as it enters our mind. We must be still long enough to listen intently to what we are thinking.

Recognizing that you are actively participating in negative thinking is half the battle won. Many people spend years in denial completely oblivious to the fact that 90% of the thoughts they allow in their mind daily are not positive. Mankind as a whole needs to realize how important our thoughts are to the quality of life we live. Mind is All and Thoughts are

Everything. It all begins with a single thought. God gave us the ability to manifest any kind of life we desire. But the first step to creating a great life is thinking about one.

It is imperative that we take time to monitor our thoughts. Begin to think of your thoughts as seeds and the Mind being the garden. The garden will produce precisely what we plant. If we plant thoughts of a stressful, sickly, impoverished life in the garden of our minds, that is exactly what we will get.

Because many of us don't realize how often we actually have negative, fear-based thoughts, conforming to this positive way of thinking may seem challenging at first. But anything you do continuously will eventually become a habit. And this is a habit that is well worth developing.

I created the simple Recognize - Reject - Replace formula to remind myself to make positive thinking a daily practice.

Recognize. The best way to clearly recognize what thoughts you are having is to slow down a little in life. We rush around from work to home and back barely having enough time to breathe properly, so of course the last thing we do is consciously monitor our thoughts. But it's a must that we take time to do it. We should create daily rituals to remind us throughout the day to focus on what thoughts we are allowing into our mind. More importantly, which of those thoughts we are devoting an extended amount of time. The first step is recognizing and acknowledging that we are indeed having negative thoughts. If the word "negative" makes you feel bad, don't use it. The practice of identifying negative thoughts is not to make you feel bad, it's to help you pinpoint the problem so you can change it. Once you have done that then you can move forward to a positive solution. Call the thoughts whatever you choose but learn to distinguish thoughts that make you feel good from thoughts that make you feel bad.

Reject. Once you have identified a negative thinking pattern, you now have the ability to reject those negative thoughts. Many spend half their lives having no idea they can reject negative thoughts. We have the power to not accept any thought that comes into our minds that isn't positive and does not make us feel good. How a thought makes you feel is the first clue to labeling it. Do you feel sad, guilty, angry, afraid, etc. when you have this thought? If so, then It can most certainly be filed away in the negative thought folder. When it returns, it will be easily recognizable, and you will not allow the thought to persist which can be detrimental to the quality of your life.

Replace. Once we have learned to recognize the negative thinking patterns and begin training our minds to reject those lines of thinking, we can then move forward to replace the negative thoughts with positive ones. This is the fun part. We have all the power here. We can choose which thoughts we allow to take up space in your mind. It truly is just that simple. After ridding our minds of the damaging thoughts, we now have clear space to fill as we see fit. We can now replace thoughts of fear with thoughts of security and courage, thoughts of hate with thoughts of love, thoughts of defeat with thoughts of triumph. That is how we become the masters of our own fate.

Sound great? Well, it's definitely an attainable goal, but when you are a baby in this new way of thinking, you are quite vulnerable. That vulnerability can feel like hopefulness and eagerness and can sometimes leave you susceptible to people who may not have your best interest at heart. Unfortunately, my strong desire to heal from my past allowed me to fall prey to many spiritual teachers who were not good people.

When you are on a spiritual journey, you come across many people who feed you information, and all of that information is not accurate. I once had a life coach or spiritual advisor whose main focus was teaching me to "transcend human emotion." As his student, I wasn't allowed to express hurt, pain, or fear because his theory was that in order for mankind to evolve to their higher selves (as he believed he had), they must transcend natural human emotion. I bought this hook, line, and sinker at first until I later started to become sad and disheartened with his teachings. Something didn't feel right. I was confused and in more pain than before I began working with him. Although I knew the benefit of not allowing yourself to stay in an unhappy state, I was struggling each week in his class with having to stifle all human emotions. It just didn't feel natural. He referred to himself as "D-Amen or Di Amen De Mere." He assured his students that he had spiritually ascended to these higher levels of consciousness and self-mastery that he was teaching us and that was the ultimate goal for all humans. He promised to take me through spiritual exercises that would finally rid me of the pain of my past. I was elated and began to feel that he was sent to me by God himself to help me heal. He told me that he was the key to my complete healing and his spirit and mine had been connected in several past lives and it was destined that we eventually came together.

I had failed in all of my past efforts to heal from witnessing the tragic murder of my grandmother, who had raised me from infancy. And at that point in my life, I was still suffering from the memory of that horrible incident. My grandmother was killed by a single gunshot womb to the head, in front of me, by my grandfather, her husband of thirty-two years. I was only seventeen years old when I witnessed this horrific incident. When I became a student of Mr. D-Amen's, I communicated to him my desire to finally heal from this particular past trauma. He assured me that he possessed the knowledge to help me, and through his guided meditative techniques I would finally be able to put it in my past. He even told me that during a deep meditation we would travel back to the day of the murder of my grandmother and change the outcome which would allow me to finally heal for good.

I started to believe he was the key to my healing and peace. I was hopeful and desperate and had put complete faith in this particular man who was a very attractive, physically fit, dark skinned, bald headed, muscular man whose day job was physical training. He and I would read and meditate privately together. We began to grow much closer; he even took me with him when he physically trained some of his clients. I wasn't even put off when he and I became physically involved, because he said due to our deep spiritual connection it was only natural that the next step for us was to connect sexually. There was not one ounce of suspicious doubt. I trusted that Mr. D- Amen had all the answers to my emotional problems.

He had been a minister once in another state and according to him he had been trained by the most reputable kemetic teachers in the "Laws of Maat." He assured me that he and I were "Twin Flames" and had been connected in many different lifetimes or incarnations as he called them. Although that concept was foreign to me, I trusted and believed his every word. Somehow, I let his divine self convince me that the female companion he lived with was not the woman he desired. I believed him when he said he and she had no spiritual connection and he had made a horrible mistake by allowing her to move from another state to be with him. He said he had lost his mental and physical desire for her. He told me that he must meditate on the correct, divine way to exit the relationship, so he would have favor with God. All while we continued our physical relationship.

Needless to say, I was naive for being so trusting, but I tell you this story because the urgent desire to heal from things that have hurt and haunted your life can make you very vulnerable. That kind of vulnerability can cloud your judgement. When I became involved with him, I had not yet fully understood my own power, the amazing power that God gave me to take charge of my own healing and initiate the steps I needed to put my past trauma behind me. I was still believing in a human being. I gave him the power and the control over my personal healing. Even when his actions in no way resembled the Divine Being he claimed to be, my desire for healing allowed me to dismiss the obvious deception and convince myself that the key to all my pain was in a man, this man in particular. This self-proclaimed master teacher of Maat'. I thought he could actually heal me for good. I was so excited to finally be rid of the suffering I had been living with for years. I was wrong, and that situation caused me a lot of pain and devastation. He was definitely no elevated being. I sincerely believed that God had sent this person to help me but I had to accept that he was simply the typical flawed male opportunist. That was a hard lesson, but in retrospect, with the state of mind I was in, I completely understand how I was misled by him. I take full responsibility for allowing myself to be reeled in. This was my fault. I didn't know that the only person that can truly heal me is me. God already placed within me all the tools I needed to repair my heart from all the trauma I had experienced. I know the truth now. It's all in my hands. I have the key to my own healing and happiness. God gave it to me at birth.

It turns out that he violated the rules of the spiritual unity center where we met by becoming personally involved with his student. As a result, he was suspended. I in no way blame the African spiritual center where he taught because they do not promote this type of behavior and they took immediate action to rectify it. However, I was left to undo the emotional damage and figure out how to assure it never happened again. I'm much stronger now, and due to the lesson learned, I don't regret a thing. It taught me that no human being can heal me. God gave us the tools we need, and it's time we all begin to use them, and that is specifically what I began to do. I learned to turn inward. I began sitting in silence more often and practicing longer periods of meditation. Doing so allowed me to truly figure out my own areas of self sabotage. I learned exactly what I was doing mentally to continue to suffer from my past. I learned to take complete responsibility for my own emotional advancement. There may be people that can guide us in our healing, but ultimately it is up to us and us alone.

Sometimes when we do not receive the love that we are meant to have from birth, we spend most of our lives looking for it in other people. Sometimes those people let us down. Whether we are aware of it or not, we look to them to fix the broken parts of us, because we have not yet learned to fix them ourselves. Unfortunately, I formed that type of relationship with one of my siblings. This relationship, although it was always based purely in love, it caused me to form unhealthy desires for approval. Because there were no parents in our lives. My need for validation came solely from my sibling's opinion of me. This unhealthy attachment prevented me and my sister from simply being sisters. Her maternal role in my life caused me to unfairly put her on a pedestal she never asked to be on, but it caused my disappointment in her to be intensified once I realized that she too was as flawed as I, and that she also had emotional issues to heal from. She processed our mother's abandonment completely differently than I did. She appeared much stronger than I was emotionally which caused me to lean on her for emotional support after the murder of our grandmother who raised us. I always felt that I needed to be perfect to be loved completely by her. I always had a fear of her walking away and abandoning me like our mother. After conversations where my issues were highlighted, I became extremely hurt and felt constantly attacked, which created distance in our relationship. Early on, I didn't realize how this dynamic affected me emotionally. Because I was so broken, I accepted it and tried to please so that I could be loved. I didn't have the courage or the strength to say, "I'm great," or "So what, I didn't do everything the way you would have, but I'm proud of me." I would not actually gain that strength until much later in my life. When I finally did, it felt wonderful.

No one deserves to feel less than anyone else. We are all amazing blessings from God. Transforming the belief that we are not as worthy as others is up to us. People will hurt and disappoint us. Most of the time they are not intentional acts. Many will go to their graves never understanding the full extent of the pain they have caused us. You have to choose not to suffer. You have to choose to forgive them whether they ask for your forgiveness or not. Learn to love the best in them even when they point out what they feel is the worst in you.

Everyone reacts and responds to others based on their own beliefs and history, which helps them form their individual perceptions of how life should be. I know beyond a shadow of a doubt that my sister loves me and has never meant me any harm. However, sometimes people can unconsciously inflict their perception of the world onto others, which can cause them great pain. Their idealistic view of the world can be forced onto others all in the name of love.

What helped me release that unhealthy attachment of needing my sister's approval was the realization that sometimes the ones causing the pain can sometimes be completely unaware of it. There may be deep-rooted underlying reasons for why they do certain things, but unless they begin the journey of self-discovery and self-mastery themselves, they may never discover those reasons. The intent behind the situation is very important. Their intent is not always to hurt. They believe they are helping you out of love. They actually love you, but sometimes they are loving and hugging you on the outside, but subconsciously hurting you on the inside. If they have not sat and dissected their own pain, that pain unconsciously transfers to the ones they love and leaves devastating effects. Those effects are not always overt and obvious. It is a subtle form of abuse that they may not have the verbiage to describe, but it can cripple the self-esteem of the very ones they claim to love. It comes disguised as love, protection and concern, making it much harder to identify for both the giver and the receiver. It can kill the human spirit, like stepping on a budding flower or slowly taking the air out of a balloon. Learning to love yourself is the only way to heal from this. Forgiving the ones who did it to you and realizing that they quite possibly had no malicious intent and meant no harm is vital in recovering from any form of abuse.

"Father forgive them for they know not what they do," Luke 23:34

There are many situations in life that if we had the opportunity to do over, we may make a different choice. Learn, grow, and move forward knowing that you are deserving of love, no matter what. No one has the right to devalue another human being. Deal with the part of other people that makes you feel good. Don't allow anyone to point fingers at you and make you feel bad about yourself. Uplift yourself and know that you did the best you could. And if you haven't, forgive yourself for that as well. Take control over your own emotional health and set healthy boundaries.

Fortunately, by the time those damaging criticisms circled back to me from my family I had developed the tools that prevented them from leaving their normal destructive blows to my self-esteem. I urge everyone reading this book to please focus on the good in others and love them without judgement. Please don't belittle them and excuse it away as concern. Love them wholeheartedly. Accept them for exactly who they are and don't berate them for their decisions that may differ from ones you feel you would have made. Life can be challenging, and people are beautifully and uniquely individual. Love them for who they are, because not doing so can cause them a lifetime of sorrow.

I kept my children very sheltered. I didn't want them out in the world for fear that they would get hurt. I used to experience extreme panic attacks about them getting hurt. Some of them resent me for keeping them so close, but it was the only way I knew how to love. Now that I have done the emotional work on myself, I realize I was operating directly from my own trauma. All of my decisions were made out of subconscious fear. I thought keeping them inside would keep them safe. My intent was not to hurt them, but to them it transferred as that. My sister's intent was to love and protect me, but it landed as harsh, critical judgement that halted my healing for years. There isn't any part of me that believes she intended to hurt me. Which made forgiveness much easier.

Blatant and intentional abuse, on the other hand, is harder to forgive, in my opinion. Overt and intentional abuse in any form is unacceptable and I encourage anyone who has endured it to seek the help you need because not doing so is compromising the quality of your life even if you don't believe it is. At some point, to achieve complete healing we must forgive that type of abuse as well. It doesn't mean we have to allow those people into our lives, but we must forgive them for our own spiritual growth. To truly live, we must forgive.

True happiness is possible, but we hold the key to our own happiness and self-worth. We must stop giving those keys to other people with the unrealistic expectation that they can save or heal us. The true healing lies in our mind, our internal thoughts about ourselves. When I deliver my speeches, I always say "Your life is like a coloring book, and only you have the crayons, so design the life you desire." Well, many times we give other people the crayons to our coloring book, giving them control over the outcome of our lives. We must take our crayons back. We must take responsibility for our own lives. We have the opportunity to color an amazing life, but we must do it ourselves. No one else can heal us. No one can make us feel worthy. No one else can make us happy. The power to do so is within us all. Who has your crayons? Who have you allowed power over your mental and emotional health? Go get your crayons back.

I now realize I have the power to Reject the negative thoughts that caused me for so many years to feel like a worthless, unwanted child. Once I was able to Recognize the damaging thoughts, I saw that I had a choice to allow my mind to focus on them or not. I assure you that not many people, if any, over the course of my life ever reminded me that my mother abandoned me. It was my own constant mental reminder that plagued my life for years. I was the one making the choice to devalue my own existence by internally belittling myself, which affected my self-esteem for years. Once I recognized and rejected the negative thinking pattern, I then had the opportunity to Replace all the bad thoughts with good ones. Recognizing, rejecting and replacing all negative thoughts will change your life as it did mine.

It may be a fact that many of us didn't have the best parents or many have lived through traumas that make it harder for us to feel that we are a valuable contribution to society, but we are. We are all valuable creations of God that have a significant purpose on earth. Everyone who has ever been born is worthy of happiness and has a positive reason for being here. We just need to do the necessary work to mentally and emotionally move forward and stop reliving our past. Adopt the "Recognize, Reject, and Replace" tool into your life so you can live up to your fullest capabilities.

Your future is bright,
But past trauma can dim the light.
We may not always get it right,
But opportunity starts over in the night.
Each day we can Win the fight,
Believing that everything will be Alright.

4-23-2020 SaBrina Fisher Reece

We are all extraordinary beings. Every single human being was placed on this earth for a reason. It may not always feel like it, but there is a positive purpose for everyone's existence. Each of us has something great to add to this world, but we must seek that greatness on our own. We try at times to remind others of their greatness and assist them in remembering that they were created perfectly by God, but they must learn it and receive it for themselves.

You, the person reading this book, are amazing! You are smart and deserving of love. No matter what choice you have made that you consider bad. As long as you wake up every morning you have the opportunity to learn from your mistakes and move forward. You are just as valuable as every human being on earth. Even the people you believe are perfect or better than you are not. We are all valuable and not accepting that value can prevent us from finding our purpose. The road to finding out what that purpose is can get blocked due to pain and trauma, but as long as we are still breathing, we all still have the chance to clear that path to greatness and eventually reach our destined purpose.

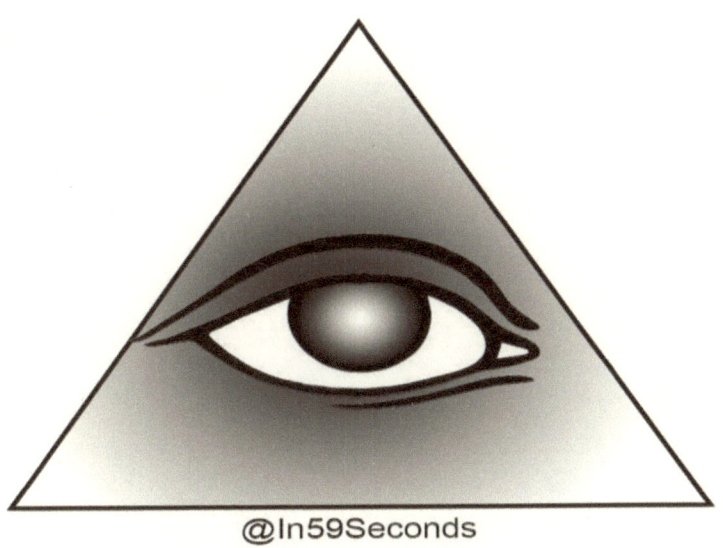

Use your mind to imagine the impossible, and it will appear.
-SaBrina Fisher Reece

Chapter 10

Spirituality and Sexuality

Being raised in the church, sexuality isn't something most church kids get to explore as teenagers or young adults. We spend so much time trying not to sin, and believing that any pre-marital sexual desires are punishable by "fire and brimstone," that we never learn that sexuality is natural. We are taught to be ashamed of our natural sexual desires.

I am writing this only a few months after my 50th birthday, and due to my childhood religious beliefs, it took me until my 40's to abandon the notion that a healthy, adventurous sexual relationship was bad. Once I became sexually active, I participated for the act of sex alone, having no idea of the mental, emotional, and spiritual connections that can occur a from closeness of that sort. No one ever told me there was an intense spiritual exchange that comes from sharing your body with another human being.

I was born a Leo, so I always refer to myself as a passionate fire sign. I have had what I call some very intense relationships. However, as I began to age and search for healing and truth, I seemed to develop an antenna for knowledge of who human beings truly are, and what our particular purpose is here on earth. Throughout this journey, it has become apparent to me that the closer I get to "truth," the more in tune I become with my own sexuality. This concept seemed weird to me at first, so weird that I didn't know how to mention it to others. But the more I studied the more I learned and the closer I became to what is described as "enlightened," the more sexual I became. I don't mean I became promiscuous. I became more in tune with my own body's sexual urges. I began to realize that somehow mind, body, and soul were all connected. Spirituality and Sexuality are somehow deeply entangled.

As my studies continued, I would read book after book and attend lecture after lecture on "being the best you can be." I would delve into the philosophies of Joseph Murphy, Eckhart Tolle, Earnest Holmes, Madame Blavatsky, Don Miguel Ruiz, Earl Nightingale, Neville Goddard, Greg Braden, Norman Vincent Peale, Zig Ziglar and many others. Inside of me there was a yearning, a hunger that I could not explain. I was looking for something deeper. As the years went by, I would continue to read and learn and one day in particular while reading a book called, "The Secret of The Ages" by Robert Collier, I came across information that seemed to resonate as truth to me. This particular information was about the power of our minds and how we all have the ability to manifest great things into our lives via the use of our minds. While reading things that I felt were the missing peace to the human puzzle my body would react. It's very difficult to explain, but when I would read a specific sentence that made a little light bulb come on in my head, it would also arouse me. I am aware how unusual this may sound, but it was indeed happening to me.

I began to yearn for someone whom I could have a stimulating conversation with and quite often found myself disappointed because the average person just lives and accepts what life gives them. I became frustrated with attempting to ask others questions like "What do you believe in?" or "What do you think your purpose is here on earth?" just to receive answers such as "I never thought about it." I would ask myself, "Well if he or she has never thought of it, why do I constantly think of it? Why am I so different? What is this urge to know more?" This burning desire for stimulating conversation made dating the "Average Joe" impossible.

Although I enjoyed drama filled Reality shows like most people during that era. I could only watch them for a short while without being drawn back to shows about the origin of the universe, Ancient Aliens or shows about mindfulness, meditation and mentalism. Whatever sparked this massive curiosity inside of me has never left.

In Chapter 12 of my book, "My Spiritual Smile," I speak about being on a plane coming from a spiritual retreat in Bali Indonesia, and the vast range of emotions I experienced all at once after reading what I believed to be a significant paragraph in a book called "The Law of Attraction-How to Get What You Want" by Robert Collier. In that chapter I explain that I felt like laughing and crying simultaneously, I felt happy and sad all at the same time. The part I left out, however, was the sexual arousal I experienced as well. I didn't know how to explain it and didn't think my readers would understand, because I didn't understand it myself. I was finally brave enough to mention it to a friend of mine named Denzell, when he accompanied me to a Toastmasters International Convention in Washington DC. I was apprehensive, but he and I had shared so many extensive conversations about life and religion that I felt comfortable enough to tell him. He was a man who had worn many hats in life, from street hustler to minister, so as he and I sat in some little eatery near the convention center in DC I began to tell him about my unexplained arousal when reading certain material. Much to my surprise, he completely understood. He explained to me that spirituality and sexuality are connected. Nothing is by chance, and there's nothing that wasn't already thought of by our amazing creator. I was so pleased to find that another human being understood this. I thought it was weird and was sort of embarrassed to communicate it, but he helped me to understand that it was actually normal. I began to further study the connection between our sexuality and our spirituality.

I have never believed in casual free sex. I have always felt that sex should be shared between two people who are connected mentally and emotionally as well as physically. However, being raised in a strict home, it took me a long while to view my role in sex as one where I deserved and should seek pleasure. As a young girl, married at nineteen, I always thought of sex as something you gave to your husband to please him.

Years went by, and a marriage or two later before I began to realize that there should be something in this for me as well. I began to learn about female orgasm after having conversations with a few friends that were a lot more sexually liberated. It still would take years before I was comfortable identifying and asking for what I needed in bed. Fortunately, by the time I started my spiritual journey I had fully embraced my own sexuality, but I definitely had no idea that it was tied to my spirituality in any way.

There have only been a limited few that I have loved deeply, and those relationships were very passionate and sexually intense. In my first book I speak candidly and in detail about my addictive relationship with my youngest child's father Phillip Clarence Morris aka D'Ablo. I spent a lot of time fighting those urges, because I did not feel that he and I had a real future together. However, I now view that involvement differently. I believe we had and still have to this day, what many would call a spiritual soul tie. The intensity of these ties is hard to understand and even harder to break. These are not always as loving and romantic as one might think, but I truly believe there are spiritual lessons to be learned from deep bonds like these.

Now that I am older, I have little or no patience for any relationship with a man that isn't attempting to evolve mentally and spiritually. He doesn't have to believe in what I believe in, but any man I meet in this second, golden half of my life that is closed minded and unwilling to at least entertain the idea that we all are human beings having a spiritual experience, can't be a part of my personal life. I would love to grow and learn with a partner. I want to stay up late deeply engrossed in stimulating conversation with my mate. I was dating someone in June of 2019 for a very brief time. Initially he appeared to be a happy open minded guy. But by the third or fourth time we got together it was obvious that not only was he stuck and very uncompromising in his way of thinking but subconsciously quite negative. I ended that swiftly. I prefer to hold out for a mate that stimulates the spiritual me.

There is only one man that I couldn't seem to cast aside as quickly as others. I love my youngest daughter's father deeply, but due to his history of street life and trauma, he was incapable of loving me the way I deserved. He has a difficult, narcissistic personality, so I never wanted to marry him, but I did have the desire to bond with him on a deeper level, especially since we shared a child. I wanted him to be a good man without having an ulterior motive. However, I think his street history robbed him of some key elements needed in a loving involvement. All his moves seemed to be calculated, manipulative ploys for control.

The hardcore life he chose to lead caused him to be quite selfish and cold hearted at times. I always knew I deserved much better than that, even from a lover. I wanted a kinder, happier man in my life, one who is positive and protective, who puts others first. A man who checks to see if you made it home. A man that calls to see if you or your children need anything. I desired the naturally loving, caring man that he was not. D'Ablo never apologized when he was wrong. He simply allowed time to pass and never addressed it. He was a horrible communicator, which is the opposite of what I wanted. Healthy communication was something that was at the top of my list of qualities I wanted in a man. I have no doubt that my choice to keep reinvolving myself with him was keeping my true king from entering my life.

Until I was fully ready to break that soul tie, I tried a different approach. Instead of repeating past behavior and putting Phill down for every negative characteristic I resented him for having, I learned to have more compassion for what had been stolen from him emotionally. I convinced myself that deep inside of him was a much better person. This caused me to develop a deeper but different love for him. I fell back in love with the phantom version of him whom I believed was buried inside. I started to feel like I had been robbed of something after knowing him for twenty-five years and having a child with him but never seeing the best of his personality. Our daughter has the sweetest, most loving personality I have ever seen in a child, so I just knew some of that goodness had to be inside of him as well. The idea that I would one day experience a different, more advanced, authentic version of him is what kept me intimately connected to him even into my early fifties.

I know that you're thinking; I was simply making excuses for him. I, too, had a difficult childhood and it didn't make me an inconsiderate jerk. It's all a choice. We are in full control of how we treat others. I just wanted to have a better story to tell our daughter. I wanted the positive memories to be real and not just fabricated stories. So I kept reigniting the same old fire. Clearly there were better moments, when I didn't think he was pure evil, but one thing I have learned is we do not have to accept 10% of someone. Once we truly develop our self-esteem we know we deserve love, kindness, generosity, and compassion 100% of the time.

My close family wasn't as forgiving of D'Ablo, and were simply sick of me painting a hopeful inaccurate picture of him. My older children hadn't forgiven him for his inconsistency as a father to their little sister, and they couldn't understand how

I had. Truth is, I thought he would change. I thought he would one day actually be the person he portrayed on his radio show. I thought he would realize that describing himself as an asshole and being proud of that was just ignorant. We can pray all day for the ones we love to be kinder, more positive, loving and more productive people, but we can't make it happen. Only they can. I attempted to do the visualization work that I believe so strongly in. I tried seeing him in a different light and creating the images and positive scenarios in my head. I do believe this can alter the outcome of situations, but I never wanted to force my will on him. I wanted him to change on his own and he never did.

Soul ties or not, I got to a point, once again, where I had given up hope that he would ever provide a different experience. I knew I did not have to accept the burden of dealing with the darker sides of his personality. The intense sexual contact between us quite often sparked feelings of jealousy. However, when I would logically pull back and think about it I knew I didn't want him for the long haul. I knew pursuing anything other than what we had would be settling. I didn't want him as a permanent mate, but I wanted him to want me in a healthy, non-possessive, non- territorial way. I'm not sure if that's normal or if it's some unresolved egotistical issues I still need to deal with.

I was grateful that I was not the one that had the responsibility of showing him a better way. I didn't have the energy to break down his defensive walls or deal with his self-serving shenanigans. It was too hard and he was too stubborn. I was happy to leave that task to some other woman and just enjoy the great sex and his beautiful smile. At least, that's what I told myself. Our sexual connection was unshakable, even into our fifties, making it seemingly impossible to deny each other that physical connection no matter how much we fought and disagreed otherwise. We couldn't seem to share the same space without somehow ending up having sex. I would tell myself that I was cool with that but I continued to yearn to know a deeper side of him. I wanted to be able to tell my daughter about the wonderful characteristics of her father, so I chose to focus on those. I always uplifted him and showed him respect and support, something I didn't feel he deserved from me. I always made him feel like he was the most handsome person in the world, hoping that my example of positive kindness would invoke the same in him. I had gone through a spiritual, emotional transformation that allowed me to live a life filled with happiness, prosperity, peace and love and I wanted that for him as well.

Make no mistake, I know my worth. It took years and a lot of emotional work to develop and authentic self-esteem. That self-esteem has been my ultimate saving grace in all of this. It has served as that final boundary that kept me from being consumed by this man, especially during times when his goal was to get me to a point of complete submission. A submission he never deserved. Why ever would I submit to a man who never had my best interest at heart?

I am aware that I'm a beautiful, successful woman. My confidence was not the issue. He believed I was too confident, so he liked to withhold compliments from me. That alone could have been quite damaging to the self-esteem of any woman. Reluctantly, I had to accept that these were malicious attempts to break me down. It was hard, and I did not want to believe that anyone wanted another person to feel bad about themselves. I would always find something positive to say to uplift him. I would try to encourage him any chance I got. He never did the same. I felt like a little puppy who needed to be patted when he walked in the door. It's shameful and embarrassing, but I pray it helps another woman move forward sooner than I did.

I was tired of the years of his pride filled, illogical disagreements and I truly wanted to know who he was internally. Yep, I was still trying. There had to be more substance to his man who had been my best friend and confidant for fifteen years before our child was even conceived. I tried to pray, meditate, light candles, burn incense, twinkle my nose and bewitch him into the person I wanted him to be. I was determined to reach inside of him and pull out this better person that I convinced myself existed. I needed this other person to exist for our daughter's sake. When she is older I don't have a problem telling her that her father was a reformed gang-banger and drug dealer, but I was not happy with possibly having to tell her that he was an insensitive, unauthentic, self-serving, manipulative asshole. I was trying to change him so he never hurt her as he had me. I had the hardest time just simply seeing the writing on the wall. He enjoyed being who he was, and he wasn't trying to change. He never thought he was wrong, he never apologized for anything. He didn't see any flaws in his personality and had no desire for spiritual evolution whatsoever, but as I grew spiritually I wanted to know him spiritually. Unfortunately, he was not ready for or had no idea how to share that part of himself.

Don't think for a second that I am not aware that this extensive chapter in yet a second book that focuses on this same involvement with this same man, means I still have some work to do. I know, but I'm happy to be transparent with you and take you on this journey with me. I know there are many women in similar situations and I pray my candidness helps them. I want others to know that even when you've gone 90% of the way with your healing and transformation, you can still find yourself struggling with that final 10% of the journey. There are lessons to learn until the very end. Hold on, stay strong. Don't become discouraged just because you have found yourself vulnerable again. There is a lesson of growth and power you will gain from each situation.

Finally I did get to the point where I was ready to fully move forward, cut all personal ties between him and I and allow him to only be a father to our daughter. I was done waiting on God to touch his soul. I was done waiting on him to apologize for his heartless bad behavior. I believe God had shown me clear signs that this man was not who he chose for me.

I believe this was one of the signs: One evening, after once again engaging in my sexual relationship with my youngest daughter's father, I was emotionally upset because I felt, once again, that I was wasting valuable time on a man I simply had emotionally evolved past. A man whose battle scars ran too deep and whose unwillingness to grow emotionally caused my level of respect for him to greatly diminish. So, unlike other times when we had rekindled our intense sexual relationship, this time was different. I felt that the choice to do so was distracting me from my spiritual path, and my soul was visibly upset by my choice. I believed our sexual attraction was an unhealthy distraction. I took my daughters to eat shortly after the encounter and my baby girl who is his daughter as well, was five years old at the time, she kept asking me "Mommy what's wrong, why are you so sad?" I couldn't explain it, nor could I shake the feeling that I had. I tried to rationalize it in my mind by asking myself, "SaBrina, what's the big deal? You have slept with this man hundreds of times. Stop tripping." My entire soul seemed unsettled and disturbed. When I got home, I simply wanted to sleep it off, so I took a Tylenol PM and had a glass of wine. That night something unexplainable happened.

    As I slept, I was awakened by some sort of spiritual vision. Please understand that for sake of communication I will call it a vision, but I honestly do not know what it actually was. I am positive I was not asleep. In the vision, my daughter's father Phill (D'Ablo) got up out of bed. I was still lying there on the right side of the bed. He turned towards me. He had on a light blue shirt and light blue pants. Directly out of his clothing, down where his genital area was, a substance began to flow out of him and towards me. It flowed out consistently like water flowing from a hose. He turned towards the door as if he was leaving the room, but he seemed to be struggling to get there. He appeared to be moving in slow motion as if he had heavy weights on his feet. It took him so long to get to the door that I fell asleep, which is why I am certain that it was not a dream.

Apparently in his struggle to make it to the door he had fallen back onto the bed with me and we both had fallen asleep. I know that we both had indeed fallen asleep because It was the sound of his snoring that woke the both of us up and started this unusual spiritual interaction rolling again. Please understand, he was not physically present in the room. He was not in the house. This imagery that I was currently involved in was not actually happening in the physical, tangible sense. When we woke up, I noticed he was still in the room and had fallen back onto the bed and fallen asleep a third time. I said, "I thought you left." This spiritual him never spoke a word. I say the spiritual him because I am aware this moment was not actually happening in real time, but his body was not translucent or ghost-like. He appeared to be solid. He got back up and headed for the door attempting to leave again. He was still moving in very slow motion, literally struggling to make it to the door as if something was pulling him back. This time he actually made it to the door. His journey towards the door must have taken a long time because I fell asleep once again. In this realm it was very clear when I was awake and when I was asleep, meaning this was not a dream. When he finally reached the door, I was awakened by the sound of his hand jiggling the doorknob. I looked in that direction and with his hands on the doorknob he turned back to look at me. In that very moment as his head turned to look back at me, a black entity rushed from his body onto mine. This black spirit seemed to paralyze the entire left side of my body. There was a knowing that is hard to explain, but somehow, I knew that I was only paralyzed on one side. The right side of my body was fully mobile.

As this powerful, heavy spiritual force sat on one half of my body, internally I asked the question, "Is this real?" No sooner than my mind finished the question, the spiritual entity grabbed me under the arm, and I could feel what felt like fingers under my armpit. It pulled me closer and leaned into me, and in my ear said "Bri, no." It seemed to be warning me and telling me not to do something. Those were the only words it spoke. It was confusing because although the spiritual entity was dark and powerful it didn't seem to want to harm me.

Being raised in the Christian church, the only thing I knew to do was plead the Blood of Jesus, which is something Christians are taught to do to protect themselves and their families from harm or danger. I tried to get the words out of my mouth. I said, "The Blood of Jesus." Initially, I could not get it out because half of my mouth could not move. The entire left side of my body was completely paralyzed. I tried again to no avail. I kept trying to push the words, "The Blood of Jesus" out until finally on the fifth or sixth attempt. This spirit lifted itself off of my body and flew away.

I have no idea what this was. Although the entity's aura seemed dark, it appeared to be warning me or possibly even trying to help me. After discussing this with my good friend Kessan, she gave me a different perspective to consider. She suggests that the spirit saying "Bri no" was the spirit telling me not to plead the blood of Jesus because he knew he would have to flee if I continued. At one point I had convinced myself that D'Ablo was possessed by the sexual spirit of an "Incubus."

What was this? Who was this? Did I conjure up this entire scene by going to bed so emotionally upset? Did the substance flowing out of his body represent the fact that we share a child? Who knows? I assumed I could easily explain it by saying God was trying to warn me to stay away from my daughter's father. That seemed like the easiest explanation, however, I believe it's much deeper than that. There is absolutely no doubt that I was not asleep, so what was that? What realm was I in? Was this a scene from a different dimension? Did his slow-motion prolonged attempts to reach the door represent that he, too, was having a hard time leaving this toxic relationship alone?

Since I share a small child with this man, I was not open to the idea that the spirit was trying to tell me that he was evil. He had never physically harmed either of us. He has never even raised his voice at me. Indeed, there were many times when being faced with the reality that he could not control me, made him emotionally distant and intentional in his withholding of love and affection, but nothing worse than that. His large ego led him to believe that I was trying to groom him into a perfect man for me, but I truly never was. I always knew in my heart that I deserved the best mate God had for me and even though I loved him dearly, I knew Phill was not it. Despite all we have been through I have always looked past that ruthless street persona and been able to see the best in him. I think the rough street life destroys a part of their soul and the people that love them suffer for it. I do not believe anyone is all evil. This spiritual vision could have been some warning to exit the relationship for good because it was a distraction for me, but to this day I have no clear explanation for what happened to me that night. However, it did reinforce my belief that there is indeed a spiritual realm.

As I conclude this chapter it is November 2020, our daughter Journey is growing fast and fortunately Phill has become a much better father. He created an organization to mentor other young men who were swept up by the streets. He adopted the name "Dr. Phill," and has created Beakon Radio as a positive platform to share his story and help others, which makes our daughter proud. She loves listening to her daddy on the radio. Many people make conscious choices to operate on the dark side, but no one is all bad. The opportunity is always there to operate in light and love but we cannot do it for them.

He and I have chosen to interact in a more productive way. I would have once described us as coming from two completely different worlds. He is an ex-convict, a drug dealer and a gang banger, then there's me. Although I was raised in Compton, right in the heart of crime and chaos, I was raised by a strict Christian grandmother, who allowed me limited access to the outside world. Phill and I experienced completely different worlds, but somehow, we both developed the same wounds. We share the same feelings of neglect from an absent parent. This is why I believe God allowed our paths to cross. I realize we both had many traumas to heal from our past, which contributed to our toxic interactions. I'm thrilled that life has softened us both. The journey towards greatness has begun for each of us. We still find it impossible to occupy the same space without acting on our extreme sexual desire, but we no longer entertain any negativity. I now believe the sexual attraction was there to sustain us until we could develop the spiritual connection. I believe this particular man's presence in my life was designed to teach me specific lessons that I need for mental and emotional growth. One day God will fully reveal to me what exactly happened that night, but until then I have learned to be kind and show only love. Love soothes the soul. Love can turn dark into light. Love heals the heart. Love trumps everything. No matter who we once were or how much pain and trauma we have endured, we can't use that as an excuse to be unkind to others. Despite life's challenges we can always return to our true God-given nature of love. We must always stay humble and kind.

SaBrina Fisher Reece

Hold the door, say "please", say "thank you"
Don't steal, don't cheat, and don't lie
I know you got mountains to climb
But always stay humble and kind
When those dreams you're dreaming come true
When the work you put in is realized
Let yourself feel the pride
But always stay humble and kind
Don't expect a free ride from no one
Don't hold a grudge or a chip here's why
Bitterness keeps you from flying
Always stay humble and kind
By Tim McGraw

Unfortunately this man was not humble or kind, yet I continuously write about him because I sincerely believe that my experience with him and the lessons learned from it have been key in my personal evolution. I believe this man was placed into my life for my spiritual growth. I refer to him as "My Mountain." Several times I have had to climb this particular mountain. Each time, I have made it to the top and firmly planted my flag so I can move forward. However, the mountain returned in a different form. Sometimes it is covered in flowers and smells great. Other times the mountain is dead and dark and has visible thorns, yet I climbed it. Those thorns have stuck me many times. I have climbed to the top and come back down, just to find the entire base of the mountain has grown in size and engulfed me, yet still I climb.

I think we cause ourselves more hurt when we develop hopes and expectations for the ones we love. We design a picture of them in our minds and when they don't show up as exactly that, we become hurt and disappointed. We try to change them. I now realize how unfair that is. Many days I wanted to reach back with every bit of strength in me and knock fire from him. I never did, but the urge to do so let me know I still had many areas within myself to work on. He was not worth my peace of mind. No one should possess the power to make you backtrack on all of the personal growth you have accomplished for yourself. Everyone has their own path to take and along that path they may hurt themselves and others. I know I definitely have, but what I have learned is, we truly have no idea what other people are experiencing within themselves. It's a personal journey, and it is not our business to know their process, nor can we force the start of their internal transformation. We must develop extreme self-love and not allow others to continuously hurt and abuse us. WE ARE THE PRIZE!

God made us all of pure love. There is love and goodness in us all. We cannot control whether or not other people reveal their kind, loving, compassionate side to the world. We can't squeeze the goodness out of them. They may appear cruel, but internally they could be battling the very demon that causes them to react that way. They may seem distant and unconcerned, but inside they are secretly praying for the skills to express themselves better. People who are hurting tend to hurt others. We don't know the mental and emotional struggles that others endure. We should just love them anyway even if it's from a distance.

I set myself up for failure when I expected Phill to be my vision of who I wanted him to be, which isn't fair. When I started to grow and transform my mindset, I expected the same growth and maturity from him. Each person has to begin their own journey of self-improvement on their own, and there is no guarantee that they will. The true meaning of unconditional love, is loving people for exactly who they are in that moment. We don't have to tolerate bad behavior, nor do we have to marry them or choose them as our life partner, but showing them that we love them no matter what could be the very thing they need to heal. I am in no way suggesting staying involved with any person who is mistreating you. The love I'm speaking of can be projected to them from afar. Pray for them. Send them positive energy, but accept that personal transformation and internal healing is personal.

The jury is still out on the spirit that came to visit me that evening, but I have always known spirits existed. My older, Texan relatives had told me stories of seeing, hearing, or feeling the presence of spirits. I was always intrigued by a story about my play aunt, Andrea, who lived on the property that I grew up on in Compton, in a back house that my Aunt SaBra used to live in. Andrea would always tell me about my father, Jesse Paul Fisher, who had died when I was ten, entering her home. She said that my father's spirit would come there looking for his sister, my aunt, SaBra Scott Lee. She said she couldn't actually see a body, but she could see footprints in the carpet. She told me that one day she yelled out to him, "Jesse Paul, SaBra does not live here anymore," and he never visited there again. I could not have been more than 14 years old when she told me that, and I have never forgotten it.

I choose not to believe in the scary, harmful type of ghosts, but I find it quite comforting to feel that some of our ancestors are still around to comfort and protect us. The possibility of them being able to give us that little nudge we need to push our lives in the destined direction is truly amazing.

We are all students, still trying to figure out how to navigate through this earthly experience. The piecing together of that puzzle still thrills me. I hold out hope that God will place a mate directly into my life who is just as eager for knowledge as I am. We can learn and grow together. We can explore the spiritual and sexual connection together. I desire a man that is naturally kind and loving. I can visualize his warm, approving smile as he securely grabs my hand. I'm still very much a hopeful romantic and I'm truly looking forward to sharing my golden years with someone who totally understands my spiritual journey because he has his own.

@In59Seconds

The mind is like water.
When it is turbulent, it's difficult to see.
When it is calm, everything becomes clear.

-Buddha

Chapter 11
Subconscious Reprogramming Made Simple

I know this may sound complicated. What the heck is subconscious reprogramming? Even better, what is a subconscious? That is definitely a question most will ask. I sure did.

Learning the definition of the subconscious and the difference between the subconscious and the conscious minds helped me to fully understand how important my thoughts were. It gave me a better understanding of the importance of the mind and what we allow into it. From as young as infants our subconscious is being shaped.

Our belief system begins to form and assign judgement to people, places and things. For example, if we are spanked as a young child for talking too much. We form the subconscious belief that talking too much is bad and we will be punished for it. Thus, we make a conscious effort throughout our lives to minimize our words.

Some of us were warned by our parents and grandparents to "beware" of sickness and disease, because many in our family had died before us of specific diseases that were believed to run in the family. Subconsciously we fear becoming sick and dying of these diseases. These fears are ingrained with-in us and most of us don't even realize we have them.

I had studied so many scientists and authors who specialize in the subconscious mind and the general consensus amongst them is that our inner world affects our outer world. So many of the descendants before us knew this fact. Why weren't we taught this from birth? If our subconscious is so critical to our emotional advancement, why isn't this information taught as early as preschool? As irritated as I was that I did not know this information early in life, I am equally as grateful that I acquired it before I died.

For years, I believed my mother who had abandoned me as a baby could heal me if she would just call and apologize for allowing drugs to consume her life. Her negative choices prevented her from being capable of being a good mother to me and my five siblings. I spent years feeling unworthy and unwanted because of her choice to abandon and abuse her children. The story I was told of her putting me into a suitcase as a three-month-old baby and closing it, leaving me for dead, haunted me for years. Knowing this fact caused me to grow up with severe self-worth issues and random bouts of depression. Her actions caused me to form the subconscious belief that I was not valuable and worthy of life. I formed the belief that if my own mother did not see value in me then no one would. This is the very belief that I would need to reprogram. Learning that this was necessary and taking the steps to reprogram that belief was half the battle won. Unfortunately, I did not begin that process until I was forty years old. I am open and transparent in my books so others can begin the healing process sooner than I did.

Throughout my life I never once remember someone approaching me and reminding me that I was unwanted by my own mother, not once. Most of the people in my life during my twenties and thirties had no idea about my past. The only time I heard that horrible story of abandonment was when I told it to myself. Inside I would say, "SaBrina, you don't deserve love because your mother didn't love you." I was the only one guilty of that. I also chose to take my mother's actions personally. She was an addict who doesn't even remember most of the horrible things she did. In no way am I excusing her behavior, but I am pointing out how we can carry hurt and pain for so many years from people who are not sharing that weight. We are the only ones suffering, and internal suffering is damaging to our mental and physical health. Suffering is a choice we do not have to make. After studying Don Miguel Ruiz's concepts on not taking things personally in "The Four Agreements," I slowly began to change my perception of her actions. Her actions were more about her and her own mental darkness than they were about me. This helped me to slowly develop self-worth. No one deserves to travel through life feeling like they do not matter, especially when those feelings are provoked by the actions of other human beings.

On June 18, 2018, my biological mother died. I did not know how to feel. For years, I would always say that I couldn't care less if she died, so I didn't expect to feel anything when I received the news of her death. On the contrary, I was suddenly struck with crippling pain. I felt it engulf me from the ground up and I could not stop it nor did I understand why it was there. I didn't love her. I didn't even know her. Because of her drug addiction I was never given the opportunity to love her. She definitely didn't love me. So why was I in pain?

Now in tears, I became angry that I was hurting. I thought to myself who hurts and sheds tears for a mother that never loved them? Who hurts for a mother that tried to kill them? What the heck is wrong with me? Why am I crying? I was mad and stuck in one place. I literally could not move. This unwanted emotion consumed me. I don't remember who I called first or how I finally moved from that position, but I did make a few phone calls. It felt unusual because all those in my life that were close to me knew that I did not have a relationship with my mother. I recall a friend telling me that what I was experiencing was called DNA pain. I didn't want it and I was resentful that it appeared even in death that my mother still had some emotional hold over me. I vowed at that moment that I would not be attending the funeral.

As the days went by, I learned about even more unacceptable abusive things my mother had done and had not made amends for. I was angry and I was happy she was dead. I began to feel grateful that I was not aware of all of the hurt and devastation she had caused our family. I was certain that God had intervened and protected me from all the facts because I most certainly would have felt compelled to confront her and force her to rectify her wrong doings. I began to feel that I had been spared from knowing exactly how evil she was. I understand to some that may sound harsh, but I have to be completely transparent in order for you to understand the dark state of mind I had to heal from.

Those feelings of gratitude were short-lived, and eventually I began to get depressed, which infuriated me. Thoughts of suicide and unworthiness returned. I had not been depressed in years. I had done so much emotional work over the years and I could not believe that this death was erasing all of that. I can only assume that there must have been a deep secret part of me that held out hope that she would finally lick all of our mental and emotional wounds and heal all of our hearts one day. I was wrong. After finding out that my mother had been in hospice care for months and was aware that she was dying, yet didn't reach out to her six children to apologize for her abandonment and abusive behavior. I was devastated all over again. I felt like all the work I had done to heal myself had been wasted.

I am not exactly sure what changed. I have no idea why I suddenly woke up one day and decided to speak at my mother's funeral. It must have been God, but I woke up one morning and decided I needed to participate in her funeral. I began communicating with my older sister and helped to arrange an obituary that was a little more honest than the one that had originally been created by my younger sister. The first line of her version of the obituary said "Shirley Ann Tillman was a great mother." What? "Are you kidding me," I thought. "Why would you write something that is a complete lie." I was not trying to be mean, but why would we ever say that she was a great mother in her obituary? She allowed me to create a more realistic version of the obituary. It wasn't my goal to bash my mother, I simply wanted to get this process over with so I could move on with my life, especially since I felt her death was putting me back at square one emotionally. I contacted some of her living relatives from Texas and asked them for true and honest characteristics of her personality. Some said she was a loyal friend, so I added that. The day of her funeral, the venue was filled with my Eastern Star sisters and Masonic brothers who all showed up for me because I needed support and pallbearers.

The service was eulogized by Bishop Reginald Black Sr., who is a great personal friend of mine as well as my Mason brother. My oldest sister, Mary, and my two younger sisters, Verdell and Kaylen (Esther Jean), were in attendance. We were not able to locate the youngest of my mother's children. Kristen Latrell. To this day I don't know how long it was before she got the news of our mothers death. My mother was a member of the Junior Blind, and many of her friends from there were in attendance. I allowed everyone who wanted to give remarks to do so before me. I began my speech with, "These tears are not for Shirley Ann Tillman, these tears are for the six babies that suffered at her hands." I turned to my sisters who were seated to the left of me and said, "I'm sorry for the distance that has been created, and the wars that have been waged amongst us by our mother." I reminded them that the source of our pain is now gone, and we are now responsible for how we interact with and love each other from here on out. We can no longer blame our mother for the lives we choose to live. "She is gone," I said. "It is now up to us to build positive productive relationships with each other and live happy healthy lives and move forward."

I realize my speech in no way resembled the typical "Everyone is going to Heaven" funeral speech. I felt it was necessary for the closure I needed to continue on and finally put this all behind me. My mother's death left me with the realization that I still had a lot of healing to do.

At times, this mental and emotional transformation process is a long one. Reprogramming negative thought patterns, especially ones left by past trauma can take a long time. That is why it's best to begin working on them as soon as you identify each one. The time spent identifying and reversing negative thinking won't be in vain. It will truly change your life for the better.

One huge subconscious belief that I had to work overtime to reverse was the fact that specific major diseases seem to run in my family. This is a common subconscious acceptance for many. Because my biological mother had diabetes, every time I experienced any bodily discomfort, I was certain it was the onset of diabetes. I no longer believe in genetic predisposition to disease.

In the book "Feeling is the Secret," by Neville Goddard, he refers to the conscious as male and the subconscious as female. He points out that the woman, being the subconscious, has no desire to change the man, being the conscious. She simply accepts him as is. The subconscious mind does not judge what we plant with our conscious actions. If you spend all of your time telling yourself that you are poor and pitiful then that is the state of mind you will remain in. The universe will create even more situations for you to feel exactly that way. You can change your state of mind.

Feeling a certain way produces that state of mind. Feeling sad will produce sadness, feeling happy will produce happiness. The minute you identify bad feelings, do everything you can to change them. Take charge of your mood.

When I read books and I find the same concepts and beliefs that I believe in today, it's always a confirmation. It makes me feel great. It confirms that I'm on the right path. It solidifies in my mind that the knowledge is real and it's not new. Many great people had this knowledge years before any of us were ever born. This knowledge is not "new aged." It's clear that many of our ancestors possessed this great information. We must always be mindful of what we are planting in our subconscious mind because our subconscious mind will produce exactly what we believe we are. If at any point we want to change the information that we are giving to the subconscious, we have to consciously take steps to create a new picture and feel the emotions related to the new positive picture we have created. Act as if the things we desire are already happening now, not in the future, but now!

It can take years to master this concept, but doing so will change your life. Hoping and wishing does not produce a happy, prosperous life. Continuously hoping and begging God for the desires of our heart is a clear representation of lack and the fact that you have accepted that limitation. Instead, mentally pretend. Believe that it is already done. Allow your prayers to be prayers of gratitude. Act as if the things you desire have already shown up in your life and soon, they will.

The mind is a magical gift from God given to us to create our lives as we choose. Embrace your Mind and its magnificent power. Whatever has shown up thus far in your life is because you have consciously or subconsciously held those thoughts in your mind. Continue to do that intentionally and you will become the master of your fate.

Success begins within!
-SaBrina Fisher Reece

Chapter 12
Effective Prayer

I sincerely believe that 90% of the people who refer to themselves as prayer warriors are missing the key elements of effective prayer. Have you ever noticed how many people you know pray endlessly for hours upon hours, yet their lives still seem to be void of the things they pray for?

I am certain that is because ineffective prayer is pointless. It's like planting a seed in a dry desert field and never watering it. Ineffective prayers are prayers to God that are followed with fear and doubt. When we ask God for something, but deep down we are convinced we don't actually believe we can have what we are asking for, the prayer is useless.

We must "believe in things unseen," despite the logical brain attempting to rationalize our desire. We must believe it's possible, and better yet, believe it is already done. The statement, "All things are possible," means just that: all things, not just the ones we've figured out how to attain. For example, you have been praying to God for a new three-bedroom home, but the minute you attempt to focus that thought and create the visual needed to manifest this new home, your logical brain says, "You don't make enough money," or "Your credit is bad," etc. These are the negative, counteractive thoughts we must not allow to persist. Cast them out and continue to visualize your desires.

Miracles are not logical. It is simply for us to plant the seed, believe that what we desire is indeed possible and move forward and let the harvest grow. It seems we counteract the things we desire by changing our minds, changing our thoughts, and talking ourselves out of all the things we are praying to God for. It's normal behavior. We have all done it, but the key is learning to recognize when your mind has begun operating in reverse so you can instantly refocus it.

The very second that self-sabotage begins, stop it!

I also believe that the effective prayers of our ancestors can protect us and generations to come. I am certain that my beloved Texan grandmother's prayers over my sister and me have shielded us from harm on many occasions. For example, I was chased out of a crab restaurant at gunpoint in 2009. I was paralyzed with fear. I remember running out the door when my knees buckled and I slammed both knees onto the hard concrete. Somehow, I got up and continued to run, still so petrified that I fell once more. The masked gunman seemed to be distracted by my running out. Although he had the gun pointed at the cashier as she attempted to comply with his demands for money, he stopped and moved his focus from her to me as I ran out the door. He turned and ran out behind me. The second time I fell onto my back on the side of the building as he walked up and pointed the gun directly in my face.

Everything seemed to be moving in slow motion. Defenseless and on my back, I stared down the barrel of the gun. Knowing that I was helpless at this point. I stared directly through the holes in the ski mask he wore and into his eyes, too afraid to even scream. It couldn't have been more than a few seconds of deafening silence, but it felt like so much longer. He didn't try to rob me for the car keys, cell phone or camera I was holding. Instead, he stared right back at me, and just from the expression in his eyes, I could see him contemplate whether or not he should shoot me. I could literally see him trying to decide. He shifted his gaze to the right, and then locked back onto me. Then, miraculously, he lowered the gun and ran off.

Of course, I can only speculate about what happened, but I choose to interpret that situation as God saying, "No, not her and not today. I still have so much work for her to do." I sincerely believe that it was God and the persistent effective prayers of protection from my late grandmother that made him walk away. Since then, I have always felt that my life was spared that day by the Divine Source because there is so much that I have to do before I leave this earth. Writing this book is one of my destined purposes. I have been walking and talking in my calling ever since.

We all have a purpose on this earth, and once you get a glimpse of yours you will rise in the morning with an unstoppable adrenaline, fueled in a way you have never experienced before.

I will always be grateful for my grandmother's prayers, for her covering me with "The blood of Jesus," as she called it.

My children often mimic me by saying, "Mom you are always talking about being 'covered by the blood.'" It's truly hilarious to watch them imitate me, and it's comforting to see how the beliefs of the ancestors transfer from one generation to the next. It was my grandmother who instilled in me the unshakable belief in Jesus Christ. As a hair salon owner for twenty-five years, I came across many clients who told me stories of their strong belief in pleading the blood of Christ over your family as well. In the mid 90's I had one client in particular whose name I don't remember, but I'll never forget the story she told me about her son being in a car with three other people. Unfortunately, his car came under fire and was shot up with over thirty-two bullets, killing everyone in the vehicle except him. She believed her son's life was spared because she pleaded the blood of Jesus over him daily, and warned me to make sure I did the same for my children. I never saw this woman after that day, but I have never forgotten that story and I have shared it many times throughout my life. Isn't it amazing how one person's story can make a lifelong impact on our lives? I am convinced that God places specific people in our paths to guide us. This story reinforced my faith in the power of belief. The lives we lead are a direct result of our primary core beliefs. This woman believed strongly in covering her children with prayer before they left the house and that could be the very thing that saved the life of her son.

There are times when horrible things happen in life, and it's vital that we have some sort of spiritual belief system, because it's during those times that our belief in that higher power will be the only way we are able to stay hopeful. It's not our place to challenge the beliefs of others. Use that energy to clarify exactly what your own beliefs are. Rid yourself of the ones that are not productive to your life.

Jamaica February 2020

In February 2020, while on a vacation in Montego Bay, Jamaica with my friends and family, we experienced something that no tourist should ever have to endure. We were so excited to arrive because we rented this huge five-bedroom villa. We had our children with us and could not wait to experience Jamaica's finest. When we arrived at this beautiful villa we were so pleased. The house was grand, and the Airbnb pictures did not do it justice. We had our own private cook and driver for the entire seven-day vacation. We could not have been happier. They even arranged for a crib for my eight-month-old grandson.

This all went downhill quickly, starting with our return to the villa on day two after a day of shopping to find a strange man there who claimed to be the new homeowner. He said he was there to see who was occupying his property. We assured him that we arranged to rent this property in December of 2019 and had paid in full for ten guests for seven days. He told me personally that his lawyer told him to throw us out, but he had decided to allow us to stay. This was very unsettling.

In the middle of this unexpected drama we were also faced with the fact that we had given the cook $360 USD to go shopping for groceries for the week and she had only purchased approximately $80 worth of groceries and refused to provide a receipt.

A series of other unacceptable things happen that resulted in us deciding on day five to move into another house that was provided for us by the previous owner at her expense, being that she felt responsible for the situation because she never informed us that the home had been sold.

When we returned home on the fifth day and packed our bags, we told the house sitter, Sean, that we were leaving and would not be staying the last two days. We were told that we could not leave. The new homeowner, His Excellency Crown Bishop Dr. Kevin O. Smith, gave the order to chain the gate and lock us inside the property. I politely asked Sean to unchain the gate and let the van in to retrieve us and our suitcases and he said, "No." He told me that I was rude for not giving him notice that we were leaving early, and that he would not open the gate because we were scheduled to leave on February 26th, and it was only the 24th. I was in shock, but once it was clear that he was not going to open the gate and we were now apparently prisoners, I began to scream and gather my friends and family. We ran down the driveway to the front gate and I noticed there was a 3ft fence that we could climb over and exit the property. Although it would not be easy because there were nine of us; five adult women, one of which was my twenty-five-year-old daughter who was two months pregnant at the time. There were also eleven-year-old twins, my seven-year-old daughter and my eight-month-old grandson.

Out of sheer disbelief, panic, and rage we climbed the fence along with several heavy suitcases with the help of Junior, our driver. We then went directly to the Coral Gardens Police Department.

I tell you this horrible story for one reason and one reason only: even during horrific times, we must attempt to maintain a positive mental attitude. We were clearly in a situation that was beyond our control, and to this day, I have no idea what their intent was by chaining us in, but I'm so grateful I acted quickly and that we all made it back to America safely.

I had to do a lot of mental work during the days immediately following the incident. I had to pray effectively to ensure we got home safely, being that we still had two more days in Jamaica before we could all fly home. My mind was a mess. I was angry and afraid. I vowed never to return to Jamaica.

Now that time has passed, I am so grateful that no one was harmed and that I learned a valuable lesson. All humans do not have the same love and compassion for women and children that we expect them to have. Because I travel so much, God needed me to know that incidents like these are possible. I was clueless.

Since I returned home, I've received so much backlash in my choice to speak out publicly about what happened to us in Montego Bay. However, it is vital to me that no tourist experience this again. Emotionally, it has been difficult. My small child and myself have had nightmares about the incident. I have to make a choice to only focus on the positive outcome, and that isn't always easy to do, but it is necessary so that we do not continue to torment ourselves with negative memories.

I believe that God protected us that day. There is so much crime in third world countries that we never learn of. I pray for wealth for all nations so that poverty does not drive human beings to harm others.

The most important lesson is that so many of us have survived horrible tragedies in life, but we all have a choice of how much we continue to suffer after they're over. Choosing to heal and move forward in no way justifies the negative actions of others, but it frees our minds and heart, so we can move forward.

The Coronavirus 2020

Ironically while writing this book, the world was hit with a pandemic. The coronavirus, a flu-like disease, is suspected to have spread from China into the United States of America. Many lost their lives, which resulted in many people being forced to retreat to their homes. The entire United States of America and many other countries were forced to quarantine themselves inside their homes. Only essential businesses were allowed to stay open and everyone was forced to wear a mask that covered their nose and mouths.

I am fifty years old and I have never witnessed anything like this. As I write this very paragraph, the state of California, where I reside, is still currently on mandatory lockdown. The streets are bare. All restaurants are closed for inside dining. The government has strongly suggested "social distancing." People are encouraged to stay six feet apart from each other at all times. Large grocery store chains are only allowing fifty people in the store at a time. Most people are walking around with gloves and masks on in fear of contracting this virus. It's definitely a historical time.

I'm very grateful I experienced this horrible time at a stage in my life where I knew the importance of positive thinking. The mass hysteria generated by this Covid-19 virus can easily challenge a person's mental strength, even for one like myself who not only prides herself on maintaining a positive mental attitude, but also teaches others the value of positive thinking. I believe it is exactly times such as these that we find out just how much mental work is still needed in those areas. These are the perfect times to prove to yourself that your positive practices actually work. That is precisely what I did. I mentally battled fear daily.

I know all too well the danger of fear. I have spent the past seven years attempting to master positive personal development skills, but there were indeed times after listening to the news, which I normally avoid, that I found myself fearful of contracting the virus. These are the times when we put those positive mental tools to practice. Coronavirus was said to have started in China and then spread quickly to Italy. Both countries were completely locked down by their governments and no one was allowed to fly in or out of them. I reside in California, so at first the victims were far away in other countries, but eventually people I knew began to contract the virus. It was frightening. I had to speak aloud affirmations of perfect health and peace continuously to calm my nerves. I even had my seven-year-old daughter say them over and over with me. In the end, I found that when the slightest panic set in, I could cast it right back out of my mind by speaking my positive affirmations repeatedly. I know the danger of persistently allowing negative thoughts. I chose to not watch the news at all. I was grateful for these tools because there were times when it became more and more difficult to reject the thoughts of fear. Americans were now being forced to wear masks and stay inside their homes. Hand sanitizer and cleaning agents were scarce. Most businesses were closed, and the essential businesses that remained open did not allow entry without a mask and six feet social distancing. Due to the quarantine and mandatory government lockdown, a huge percentage of people had lost their jobs. People were afraid. It was definitely a challenging historical time. I had to constantly speak perfect health and abundant wealth over me and my family. It became vital to maintaining a positive state of mind during that difficult time.

I believe it is important not to waste time ridiculing ourselves for having thoughts of fear but instead see that as an opportunity to reverse those thoughts. We must acknowledge the thoughts of panic and fear before we can change them.

Instead of allowing myself to feel that I was failing at something I believed so strongly in, I began to applaud myself for having the good sense to acknowledge and identify the negative thoughts so that I could replace them with good ones. I used that crucial time to practice staying positive. I consciously chose to view the quarantine as an opportunity. The bulk of this book was completed during that time. Something inside of me felt that this pandemic was a time for people to be still and quiet their minds. I felt that doing so would produce wonderful things. What seemed to be a horrible, negative circumstance would, in the end, be positive. There was some good to come. Personally, the time at home allowed me to become more grateful and appreciative for my home. Not being able to go into clothing stores and shops or go to restaurants made me realize how easily we can do without certain things we were positive we needed. I learned to break attachments to certain things. I started to appreciate the simplicity of life. Due to the schools being closed I developed a deeper patience for my small child. I believed the world would evolve as a whole when this was all over. I was determined to use that time to create and tap into my intuitive side and come out of it more successful and more in tune with my inner self than before.

The Missing Piece to the Puzzle

My birth mother was a drug addict. She gave birth to six children: five girls and one boy. All of the children were either sent to foster care or raised by relatives. The oldest, my sister Mary and I who were born in 1968 and 1969, were fortunate enough to be raised by our paternal grandmother. Our younger sister, Verdell, was born in 1975 and was left in a hospital by my mother immediately after birth so she was raised by her biological father and his wife. The youngest two girls spent a few years in foster care, but were the only two children that my mother attempted to raise, so they have the most experience in directly dealing with our birth mother. Unfortunately, during most of that time our mother was still incapable of proper parenting, which led to even more abandonment and abuse. Right in the middle of the five female children was a son, born on May 13, 1972. We never knew much about him or his father, but we were always told his father was a dark-skinned man born in Cuba. As a very young girl, possibly seven or eight years old, I remember my grandmother taking my older sister Mary and I to meet him while he was in a foster home. I have always held on to a vague memory of that and I remember seeing a picture of him when he was four years old wearing a yellow jacket. Those memories were what I held onto for years. As I got older I began searching for him. I went to the department of social services to see if they could help because they were able to locate our sister, Verdell, and that ended up being how we all met her when she was sixteen years old. Although social services did indeed have records of his birth, foster care and legal adoption, the records were classified, because it was what they refer to as a closed adoption. They would not notify him that a sibling was looking for him so as to not disrupt his life. They allowed me to leave a note in his file saying I was searching for him, but they could not contact him. If he were to ever come looking for the information, however, it would be there waiting for him.

In 2013, I posted several times on Facebook that I was searching for my biological brother, Maurice Gonzales. I didn't know if the adoptive family had changed his name. I contacted over fifty people with the same name as my brother, but no one ever responded. I became discouraged, and eventually moved on with my life, remembering his existence throughout the years. I remember considering hiring a private investigator, but I never got around to it.

April 2020, while most of the world was on mandatory quarantine due to the coronavirus outbreak. I logged on to my ancestry.com profile, which I had not logged onto since 2013. I was quite surprised that I actually remembered the password, but I did, and was put right into an unfinished family tree that I had started working on years prior. It already had quite a bit of information and pictures. As I was attempting to familiarize myself with how to navigate the website again, I noticed that someone had created a profile for a man named Leon Gonzales, which is the name of my brother Maurice Gonzales's father. I sent that person, whose name was Michelle, a private message asking how she knew Leon Gonzales and if she also knew his son Maurice Gonzales. I briefly explained to her that Maurice Gonzales was my long-lost biological brother. I went to bed and didn't think anything of it.

The next day, I logged back in and was surprised to find that Michelle had responded. She said she knew my brother and that he goes by the name, "Mo." She told me she had done a DNA test and searched for him, and had connected his birth parents, Shirley Ann Tillman and Leon Gonzales. I could not have been happier, but I was skeptical, and wanted to be sure this was true before I got my hopes up.

In a separate message she informed me that she knew exactly how to locate my brother. She said he was living with a friend named Roy Taylor, and that she would try to contact them. I could not wait, so I logged onto Facebook and searched for Roy Taylor in San Bernardino. I sent out two messages and within fifteen minutes, one of the Roy's responded. He told me that my brother was indeed with him, and that he would have him call me. I sat there in complete shock, still uncertain if this was all real. Ten minutes later I got a phone call from a number with a 951 area code. It was my brother.

I remember feeling in that moment afraid to allow myself get excited on the off chance it was a game or trick, but it was not. It was my little brother, whom I had dreamed of finding my entire life. Maurice Gonzales was alive and speaking to me on the phone. I became very emotional; I could not believe it. I told him how long I had been searching for him. He told me that his name was Maurice William Gee. He had been given the middle and last name of his adoptive father. We spoke for approximately twenty minutes, and he gave me the cell phone number of his adoptive mother and asked me to call her.

I was hesitant because I didn't know how she would feel, but I knew I had to call. I left her a detailed voice message. She called me back and I spoke to her and her husband for over an hour. They told me how they went about adopting Maurice. The adoption was final on his fifth birthday, May 13,1977. His mother told me how happy and charming he was as a little boy. His father, William Gee worked for the sheriff's department. They loved him and wanted him. He was raised with four other siblings, three brothers and one sister. After an extended conversation with his older brother, Charles, I concluded that he seemed to have had a great life. He was wanted and loved by the family he was adopted into. His brother told me he was a very competitive person and a great athlete. His mother later sent me several pictures of him as a child, including some of him in his childhood football uniforms.

I spent two days collecting pictures of him and sharing them with my sisters and other family members. Knowing that he was alive and had been raised in a loving home brought joy to my heart.

On June 18, 2018, at the funeral of my biological mother, in my closing remarks, I said "We will find our brother, who has been missing from our lives forever." Little did I know that less than two years later those words would become a reality. I spoke it into existence. Many times, I said, "Finding my brother would make a great ending to my book." That prophecy has been fulfilled. As of today, I have not actually met with him yet, but I'm eagerly awaiting the day that I can hug my little brother and begin the journey of getting to know the man he is today.

Words are powerful, more powerful than we can ever imagine. Believing that we each have the power to create the life we choose is the ultimate awakening. God has instilled amazing greatness inside of us all. No matter who we are, where we were born, or under which circumstances we came into the world, we are all great and we each have a purpose here on Earth. Even when we are faced with life's challenges, as long as we have breath in our bodies, we still have an opportunity to design a magnificent life. It is never too late to start taking control of your life and to begin using your god given instincts and tools to guide your life in the direction you want.

Some would say that my life was hard. Being unwanted, witnessing tragedy, and experiencing great loss. I say each one of those life experiences shaped me into a woman that never gave up. I became a person who was determined to be happy, no matter what. I was determined not to allow my past to affect my future. I learned the value of my own mind, and began to manipulate and train my thoughts to mirror what I wanted in my life. That is what I desire for my readers. No matter what you have experienced in your past. True happiness is attainable. All the things that you desire for your life are indeed possible. With proper use of your mind, you can have joy, peace, love, great health, success, prosperity, and more, as long as you realize that you are the key to it all. You are an extraordinary being, and your ever-expansive Mind is Magic!

SaBrina Fisher Reece
www.SaBrinaFisherReece.com

Phone: 323-253-4313
Email: In59Seconds@yahoo.com

Instagram:
@in59Secs
@SaBrinaFisherReece
@Inspire_Me_Bri

Twitter:
@In59Seconds

Facebook:
Speaker SaBrina Fisher Reece
Author SaBrina Reece
SaBrina Speaker Reece
Inspire Me Bri

LinkedIn:
Speaker SaBrina Fisher Reece

www.ingramcontent.com/pod-product-compliance
Lightning Source LLC
Chambersburg PA
CBHW030906080526
44589CB00010B/163